The Great War
and the Romanians

Notes and Documents on World War I

Nicolae Petrescu-Comnène

The Great War
and the Romanians

Notes and Documents on World War I

With a Foreword by
General Mircea Chelaru

The Center for Romanian Studies
Las Vegas ◊ Chicago ◊ Palm Beach

Published in the United States of America by
Histria Books, a division of Histria LLC
7181 N. Hualapai Way
Las Vegas, NV 89166 USA
HistriaBooks.com

The Center for Romanian Studies is an independent academic and cultural institute with the mission to promote knowledge of the history, literature, and culture of Romania in the world. The publishing program of the Center is affiliated with Histria Books. Contributions from scholars from around the world are welcome. To support the work of the Center for Romanian Studies, contact us at info@centerforromanianstudies.com

Second Printing, 2022

Library of Congress Control Number: 2020945313

ISBN 978-973-9432-16-0 (hardcover)
ISBN 978-1-59211-093-3 (paperback)
ISBN 978-1-59211-193-0 (eBook)

Contents

Ferdinand I, King of Romania, 1914–1927

Foreword
Faith in Victory

Why republish this book, today, so many years after its initial publication in 1918?

The author, Nicolae Petrescu-Comnène, was a career diplomat who became Romania's minister of Foreign Affairs in 1938. He wrote this book at a dramatic time in Romanian history. In December 1916, the Romanian army, after a lightning advance into Transylvania, was forced to retreat due to the inactivity of the Entente forces on the other European fronts, and to withdraw from Wallachia and Bucharest. The government, the parliament, and the other state institutions retreated to Iaşi. Behind the front lines which defended a free Moldavia, a decisive battle was underway to rebuild the army. To resume the struggle for liberty and unity. To overcome the unfortunate circumstances of the times and the weaknesses of men. The result of this effort was the "Golden Triangle" in the summer of 1917 when the Romanian army, supported by France and Russia, won memorable victories at Oituz, Mărăşti, and Mărăşeşti. In those battles the Romanian nation displayed its defining qualities: courage and perseverance in pursuit of its ideals, self-sacrifice, heroism, and the will to overcome the hardships of the times. Because of these qualities they were victorious and they will always be victorious.

Nicolae Petrescu-Comnène wrote this book immediately after the "Golden Triangle" was created. Despite the victories it achieved, the international situation — the armistice (October 1917) followed by the separate peace (March 1918) of Russia with the Central Powers — forced Romania to abandon its struggle temporarily. Petrescu-Comnène's purpose was to demonstrate to international public opinion the justice of

Romania's struggle for the unification of all the territories inhabited by Romanians and, at that time, under foreign domination. Although confronted with these temporary setbacks, he did not hesitate to manifest his faith in ultimate victory. He knew that victory belongs to those who believe in it, are prepared to achieve it, and who are not afraid to sacrifice to realize it.

The book includes a speech at the Sorbonne by French Minister Albert Thomas, an eyewitness to the historical efforts at that time by the Romanians to fulfill their national ideal. He expresses the same strong faith in victory which guaranteed then the alliance between the Western powers of the Entente and Romania and has remained until today the basis of Romanian foreign policy.

The faith of Petrescu-Comnène was validated by history because it was historically justified. In December 1918 the historical Romanian lands of Bessarabia, Bucovina, and Transylvania united together with their mother country thanks to the application of the principle of the self-determination of nations and the national will of the Romanian people.

This book is republished as a historical document. It is a testament to the unbroken faith in victory of the Romanian nation. It serves today, in difficult times, as a memento, to remind us that nothing can stop a nation prepared to sacrifice to attain its ideals of unity and independence. These sacred Romanian values remain as a fundamental basis for national revival and progress.

The reader will find in this book a significant episode which served as the occasion for Albert Thomas's speech at the Sorbonne. The battle flag of the great fifteenth century Romanian prince, Stephen the Great, which was found by French troops under General Sarrail in a monastery at Mount Athos in 1916, was returned to Romania by its allies as a sign of eternal friendship. It was a symbol of faith and hope in victory for the realization of Romania's rights. It remains today, as it was then, as symbol of the national aspirations of unity and prosperity.

General Dr. Mircea Chelaru
Chief of Staff of the Romanian Army

Foreword to the 1918 Edition

Paris, 30 July 1917

Dear Sir,

I have read, with great interest, the manuscript of your book that will be published as *The Great War and the Romanians* and I would have been pleased, if I had enough time, to write the preface.

But my urgent business, which does not allow me any spare time, forces me to send you instead the speech that I delivered on 28 July 1917, when Romania received the flag of Stephen the Great, which was discovered at the Bulgarian monastery of Zugravu and sent to France by General Sarrail.

You will observe, in these few words, the admiration and sympathy that the effort of the Romanians during this war has inspired in me, and, perhaps, you will not consider them unworthy of being printed on the first pages of a work that explains and comments upon this effort with so much competence and talent.

Please receive our true and honest regards,

A. Thomas

Speech of Mr. Albert Thomas, Minister of Armaments and War Production, on 28 July 1917 at the Sorbonne, during the ceremony where Romania received the flag of Stephen the Great, found by French troops at the Zugravu Monastery (Mount Athos) and sent to France by General Sarrail:

Mister President of the Republic,
Mister President of the Senate,
Mister President of the House of Deputies,
Mister Minister of Romania,
Ladies and Gentlemen,

With great emotion and pride, I join here with the government of the republic in handing over the flag of Stephen the Great to the representatives of the Romanian government and the Romanian nation.

This flag is the symbol of VICTORY.

Yes, it is the symbol of our well-paid for victories, it represents all our sacrifices and suffering. It is the symbol of Romanian heroism, which has forever been a chief characteristic of your nation.

The chroniclers tell us how the flag of Stephen the Great arrived at the monastery of Zugravu.

Stephen the Great had been defeated in the battle mentioned here earlier by General Malleterre[1] and after his enemies had entered Romanian territory, Stephen the Great, who was recognized even by the Poles as the leader of the Christian alliance against the Ottomans, had to retreat. He went to the high valleys of Moldavia and arrived in front of the fortress of Hotin.

His mother was there and when Stephen the Great wanted to enter the fortress, she said: "I won't open this gate until you defeat your enemies, because if you are not able to beat them in the field, there is little chance that you will resist them here. The bird dies in its nest. Go, take your army and victory will be yours."[2]

---

[1] The battle of Războieni in 1476.

[2] This, in fact, is a legend concerning the fortress of Neamț. It is only a myth as Stephen's mother was already dead at the time of his war with the Turks in 1476, to which the speaker is referring.

Stephen the Great went to Voroneţ, where the monk Daniel lived.[3] He knocked on the door and the monk answered: "Prince Stephen, wait at the door because I'm praying." After he finished his prayers, Stephen said: "My army is defeated. Do I have to surrender the country to the Ottomans?" "No," said the monk. "Promise that you will build a monastery for Saint George and you will win."

The chroniclers say also that Stephen the Great took confession, prayed to God, and fell asleep. In his dreams, Saint George came to him and said: "Stephen, trust me; don't be scared, gather your army, go to fight and you will win."

In the morning, Stephen gathered his army and defeated the Ottomans.

Alter the battle he sent the icon of Saint George, the one that he always carried in battle, to the monastery of Zugravu, along with two flags of Saint George. One of these flags is here before you.

Ladies and Gentlemen,

In all of Romanian history we could not find a better example than the life of this prince who, for 47 years, fought against the invasions of the Ottomans, the Poles, and the Tartars.

The chronicler Grigore Ureche said: "Stephen the Great was one of those who was not easily defeated. In his most difficult moments, he always found the strength to rise above."

And you, our Romanian friends of the twentieth century, stood up to the conquerors, and even today we can hear the Romanian guns that will soon help bring future victories.

Please, let me share with you my unforgettable memories of my trip [to Russia and Romania in the spring of 1917].

Certainly, I saw many things. I saw a nation that desires its liberty and which has earned the right to benefit from our trust and hopes. I saw heroic leaders who, step by step, are rebuilding their most important national structures.

But of all my memories, the best are those from Romania.

There I saw the city of Iaşi in the spring: I saw the king and queen, the national monarchy around which the government rallied to save the

---

[3]This is, in fact, a reference to Daniel Sihastru. who lived at the monastery of Putna. The monastery of Voroneţ was built in 1496, long after these events.

country; a dynamic Council of Ministers, ministers who, during the moments of crisis, unified all the parties to guarantee national security.

Your parliament, Mr. Minister of Romania, has made an extra effort to succeed in its dual mission to defend the state against the enemy and to make bold reforms: introducing the universal vote and agrarian reform.

Finally, what I want to evoke here, before you, is the image of the admirable Romanian army, remade today.

Yes, Romanian brothers, we know what you went through in the autumn of 1916. We have all seen on our maps the passing of the German troops through the Carpathian valley and their attempts to surround your army.

I have emotionally lived the moments of the withdrawal of your troops, and, after this defeat, the disease and hunger faced by both the population and the army.

And, when we all thought that you were completely crushed and that you would never again become an active force, you and your army rose to the occasion.

I have seen your army marching in front of the king. I have seen it in action. I have heard the sound of our 75mm cannons. I have seen our guns from St. Etienne in the hands of Romanian soldiers, and all the other military equipment we sent admirably used. I have seen Romanian soldiers wearing French helmets on their heads, with an exquisite bearing, and I have heard General Berthelot saying words of the highest praise to your soldiers, words that only a French general could say to an army: "Look at them, how full of energy they are!"

Ladies and Gentlemen,

Romania's great effort makes us love her all the more.

France has always appreciated and tried to help those nations that fought for independence and unity. Only a few weeks ago we paid tribute, in one of our Socialist sections, to one of our comrades who fell on the field of honor. We were gathered together there, workers and Socialists, and one of the speakers told us not only about France's purposes in this war and the reunification with Alsace and Lorraine, but also about the struggles for independence that are going on at the same time and which make this Great War so grandiose. He spoke about Serbia, Belgium, and Romania. I would have wished that those in our country, who think that our nation is too tired of war, could see how enthusiastic the working people of Paris were about the idea of independence. Yes, dear Romanian friends, we love you; we have said it today, but we also love you for other reasons. We love you for representing Latinity, there, on the great eastern frontier of the conflict. We love you like brothers because we remember our Romanian deskmates from high school, we remember that in this Sorbonne we lived the years of our youth together with our Romanian friends. But we must go to Romania to understand that our friendship is not only a formal one, but that the brotherhood between our nations is very deep.

When I arrived, after crossing the Russian plain, after meeting with the Russian troops in the Carpathians, I met an agent of the Romanian Customs checking passports and baggage. Jean Richepin said what we already knew: "He's one of ours." This is what we felt hearing that man speak French like a person from Marseilles.

Further on during our trip we arrived at a peasant wedding, where the people were wearing national costumes. We stopped.

The peasants recognized the uniforms of the French officers: they acclaimed us, in Romanian of course, but we could also hear someone who said: "Long live France!"

At a window there were some beautiful girls that, seeing us, said: "Where are you going? To Iaşi? Take us with you." The entire atmosphere reminded us of our home, France. That is why, dear friends, because you are our Latin brothers, France will happily fulfill its duty to assist you. This mission, even if we did not feel the way we do about you, is France's duty. We must not to abandon you because, if we did, we would not be French.

Mr. President of the House of Deputies,

You were right when you said that in the nineteenth century the principle of nations often turned against French traditions and interests. We must remember that sometimes France, wanting to respect this principle, had to overcome much greater difficulties. But for France it was an honor to defend the idea of human rights. France wants its reunification with Alsace and Lorraine, not because they are lost territories, but out of respect for the rights of peoples, and out of its desire to liberate all territories found in a similar situation as that of Alsace and Lorraine. Nothing can stop France from fulfilling its objectives of liberation and unification. France wants to teach to the world the ideals of the French Revolution which were opposed to the German tradition of dominating other nations. France has no hesitation about supporting the right to freedom of other nations. Although in the past, due to the conditions of the time, it has not always been possible to defend these rights, other nations still trusted France and looked to her. During the nineteenth century, France helped nations that sought their political or intellectual freedom. Even today we respect those traditions and fulfill the same duty.

We can all say Stephen the Great's beautiful prayer written on his army's flag: "Oh, great St. George," said Stephen the Great, as do we today, "Oh, Liberty, you who always succeed, you who during difficult times provide us help and give us strength, you who bring to those who suffer great joy, receive our prayer to uphold these ideals in this century and during the following ones, so that we may serve you forever."

And as France and Romania are united today in this sad struggle, they will remain, beyond our future victories, forever united, to serve you, oh, Liberty!"

Preface

Austro-German propaganda succeeded so well in denigrating Romanian politics after 1914 that even nowadays there are many honest people in neutral countries who dispute the rights of the Romanians.

Certainly, this clear and precise book by Mr. Comnène will succeed in informing and persuading all readers of good faith concerned only with the knowledge of the truth. After reading these enlightened and revealing pages, the readers will no longer doubt the honesty of the Romanian patriots who assert that their aim in this war is the liberation of their territories and not the conquest of a foreign land.

The conquerors! These are Romania's enemies. The Hungarians who, anxious to participate, together with the German minority in Austria, in the Austro-Hungarian exploitation, with a view to the already known results.

For a long time, an imaginary aura of gallantry and liberalism have adorned the foreheads of Hungarian statesmen. Their status, modified as a result of the events from 1848, from the point of view of the superficial observers, could not hide its own origins. Furthermore, the Magyars, with so much ability, exploited in France and Great Britain the legend of their generosity and "their Western spirit." Their agents in the West, even before the war, discreetly let it be understood that the pan-Germanic war would not break out because of the opposition of the government in Budapest, which would temper the Triple Alliance.

But the course of events was totally different. Count Istvan Tisza, the head of the government in Budapest, more than anyone else, even more than the German sovereigns and statesmen, pulled the strings to produce the present-day dispute.

The tyrannical policy of the Magyar oligarchy acted in prejudice of Romania, of its monarchy, more than to some other nation. That's why Romania had to intervene, by all means, to protect the Romanians that were living under the Magyar yoke and suffering from national humiliation.

When the time came, Romania intervened with such enthusiasm that, in reading this book, we should not have any doubts about it. Was Romania ready to participate? Unfortunately, we have some doubts about that, and Mr. Comnène suggests that some mistakes were made.

The biggest culprit in this terrible matter is Russia, in fact the criminals who took power in Petrograd and who betrayed Romania to the benefit of both Vienna and Berlin.

It has already been proven that Stürmer, the prime minister and confident of the former emperor of all Russia, "sabotaged" Romania's campaign to assist a brilliant action of the Austro-German army to end the World War.

Has such base treachery ever been known before in world history? The traitors in Moscow will never pay enough for their frightfully cruel action against this country and its civilization.

The young Russian democracy should realize the debt it owes to Romania and the fact that they should pay it off as quickly as possible.

The Romanian leaders, the Romanian Army, and the Romanian people are worthy of the admiration and confidence of the world. We should respectfully bow down to King Ferdinand of Romania, who knew to control and overcome his instincts and also personal friendships, to carry out, steadfastly, his duty to his nation.

Invaded, plundered, and starved, the Romanian population has suffered terribly; but, just like the Belgians and Serbs, the Romanians never doubt their future liberation. They are looking to their enlightened future that will satisfy their national claims, to the detriment of the enemy of humanity.

Russia is already recovering and American troops are landing in France. The Belgian saying will come true, which forecasts "the time will come when everything will have to be paid for."

The brilliant statesman Take Ionescu said: "I don't understand why the citizens of a small state do not see that the authors of the ultimatum to Serbia and the invasion of Belgium indubitably are their enemies."

I repeat, just like Take Ionescu: "I don't understand, either." But I take consolation in the thought that there are many Swiss people who "understood."

And I still believe that the number of people that "understand" is increasing every day.

Maurice Muret
Morges, July 1917

Author's Introduction

There are many people in Europe that still do not understand the significance of Romania's intervention in the war on the side of the Allies and who are unaware of Romania's war aims. The enemies of this country, in a deliberate effort to distort the truth, have tried, over the course of several months, to convince the world that Romanian policy is one of conquest and much more, accusing Romania of having declared war on Austria-Hungary for the sole reason of hoping to participate, unfairly, in the inevitable break-up of the Hapsburg Empire.

Being part of these events, I intend to show, in the following pages, which are the real causes that compelled Romania to join in the European war, as well as the contribution it has made to that effort.

Meanwhile, I intend to demonstrate the loyal policy of the Romanian government, even from the beginning of the European crisis, and how Romanian claims are justified, being motivated by historical, political, and juridical reasons. Even now, we could say that Romania's policy was not only derived from its national claims, but also, to use Aristide Briand's expression, because "the people and their upbringing create affinities, the equal concern for justice, and also the unity of aspirations toward the same ideal of freedom and justice."

The Romanian government minutely presented its position, precisely in its declaration of war on Austria-Hungary. To enlighten readers, it is necessary to reproduce the entire text of this historical document:

> The alliance concluded between Germany, Austria, Hungary, and Italy was, as results from the declarations of their respective governments, first of all, of a conservative and defensive nature. Its main purpose was to defend the Allied states against any attack from the outside and to consolidate the situation created by the previous

treaties. Trying to adhere to its policies and peaceful intentions, Romania joined this alliance.

Devoting itself to its own internal reconstruction and trying to maintain order and a balance of power in the lower Danube region, Romania has never stopped contributing to the maintenance of peace in the Balkans. The last Balkan war, which destroyed the status quo, forced Romania to adopt a different position. Its intervention in that conflict brought about peace sooner and restored the balance of power; it was content with only a bounder alteration that made it more secure against any future aggression and also redressed the error made to its detriment at the Congress of Berlin.[4] But, following this objective, Romania was disappointed at the attitude of the cabinet in Vienna that was not what Romania had the right to expect.[5]

When the present war broke out, Romania, just like Italy, refused to join Austria-Hungary in its declaration of war because it had not received proper notification from the Vienna cabinet. In the spring of 1915 Italy declared war on Austria-Hungary and, from that moment on, the Triple Alliance no longer existed.

The political reasons that had compelled Romania to join this political alliance also disappeared. Instead of a group of states that, through their common efforts, were supposed to work together to maintain peace and the balance of power established by many treaties, new forces appeared that were at war with one other, with a view to modify all the old agreements that had formed the basis of that alliance.

These profound changes were obvious evidence for Romania that by joining the Triple Alliance its goals could not be achieved and that it should direct its attention and efforts in other directions; even more, Austria-Hungary's actions posed an ominous threat to the essential interests of Romania, as well as to its legitimate national aspirations.

Confronted with this radically changed situation in relations between the Austro-Hungarian monarchy and Romania, the latter took the liberty to act.

---

[4] The document is referring to Romania's acquisition of the territory of southern Dobrogea, known as the quadrilateral, from Bulgaria at the end of the Second Balkan War. This territory was restored to Bulgaria in 1940.

[5] The Second Balkan War was started because of the intrigues of the Austrian minister to Sofia, Count Tarnovsky, preventing Romania and Serbia from making peace with Bulgaria.

The neutrality of the royal government, as a result of a declaration of war that was not in accord either with its desires or its interests, was adopted based on the guarantees of the Austro-Hungarian government that the declaration of war on Serbia did not at all imply an effort to conquer new territories. But these promises were never kept.

We are today in a situation that might result in important territorial changes and may cause political changes that could represent a great danger to Romania's future and security. The pacifist policy that Romania, devoted to the spirit of the Triple Alliance, has strived to maintain was not understood by the people who were supposed to support her and to defend her.

By joining, in 1883, the group of Central Powers, Romania could not by any means forget the blood relations between the people living in the kingdom's principalities and the subjects of the Austro-Hungarian monarchy. It saw the friendship and alliance established between the three great forces as a guarantee for its internal peace, as well as of our common frontiers. But it knew how dissatisfied the Romanian population was with the existing situation, which strained the relations established between our two states.

Our expectations concerning our adherence to the Triple Alliance were betrayed. For over thirty years, the Romanians living in Austria-Hungary have not seen any kind of reform, even superficial, to satisfy them; they have been treated as an inferior nation, condemned to bear the tyranny of a foreign element that constitutes only a minority among the many component nationalities of the Austro-Hungarian state. All the injustices that our brothers have been subjected to have caused a continuous state of strained relations between our country and the Hapsburg monarchy, which only with great sacrifice could the royal government keep under control.

When the present war broke out, we hoped that the Austro-Hungarian government would be convinced, in the last moment, how important it was to stop urgently this injustice that was dangerous not only for our friendship, but even for the normal relations that were supposed to exist between our two neighboring countries.

After two years of war, the Romanians understood that Austria-Hungary, hostile to any kind of internal reform that could improve the situation of the subjugated peoples, was not only willing to sacrifice them, but even incapable of defending them in case of a foreign attack.

This war, that has involved almost all of Europe, emphasizes serious problems which affect the national development and also the existence of states. Striving both to contribute to the urgent cessation of the war and to defend its national interests, Romania has to join those who are able to secure its national unity.

For this reason, from this moment, Romania considers itself to be at war with Austria-Hungary.

Bucharest, 27 August 1916, 9 p.m.

Signed: E.M. Porumbaru [Romanian minister of Foreign Affairs]

This document very clearly shows the reasons for Romania's intervention in the war:

1) National unity: the liberation of the Romanians in Transylvania and other Romanian provinces that are under Austro-Hungarian domination.

2) General European principles: the triumph of the principle of liberty and justice over "force," to defend universal, political, economic, social, and religious principles.

Consequently, it is absolutely necessary to note from the beginning of this summary the idea "that the Romanian nation has not joined the Allies in this war for motives of conquest; their only purpose was to liberate Romanian territories subjugated by Austria-Hungary, to liberate the Romanians, and to unite them with their country.[6]

Do these words express the truth? Are the Romanians from Hungary really subjugated by the Magyar nation? Does Magyar behavior justify the revolt of people in Romania? These are the questions that we will analyze, succinctly, in the first chapter of this historical sketch.

The second chapter will be dedicated to the evolution of public opinion in Romania concerning Germany and its politics.

In the third and fourth chapters we will discuss Romania's participation in the war; finally, in the fifth chapter we will show which is, in our modest opinion, the fate of Romanian nation.

Nicolae Petrescu-Comnène

---

[6]Sec the declaration of 7 June of last year, made at Petrograd by the Romanian prime minister, Ion l.C. Brătianu, to a reporter from the *Petit Parisien* newspaper.

The Great War and the Romanians

Notes and Documents on World War I

Dedication

To France,

The first, who, with the sword in hand, defends the principle of nationalities, these sad pages that describe the sufferings and aspirations of a whole nation.

Gratefully, with sincere admiration,

N.P.C.

Chapter I

The First Reason for Romanian Intervention: The Plight of the Romanians in Austria-Hungary

The Situation of the Romanians in Austria and Hungary
A Brief History

The Romanian nation today[7] is an ensemble comprised, in round numbers, of 14,000,000 people, of whom approximately 8,000,000 are living in the territory of the Kingdom of Romania, 4,000,000 in the provinces occupied by the Austro-Hungarian monarchy (Transylvania, the Banat of Timișoara, Crișana, Maramureș, and Bucovina), 1,200,000 in Bessarabia, occupied by Russia, and 500,000–600,000 are scattered throughout Macedonia, Serbia, Histria, etc.

This nation forms a compact group, of great importance due to its number and qualities, in the region defined by the Dniester River, the Black Sea, and the Danube and Tisa rivers.

This territory is roughly the area of the ancient kingdom of the Dacians, conquered by the Roman legions of the Emperor Trajan at the beginning of the second century A.D. The Romanians, as their name indi-

---

[7]At the time the book was written, in 1917.

cates, are the successors of both the Roman colonists and the native population which was completely Romanized.

The colonization of these regions was not, as was believed for a long time, only the work of Emperor Trajan. Today we possess evidence about the immigration of Latin peasants to Dacia long before the time of Trajan's wars, because the fertile soil of the both Danubian and Panonnian plains offered them better conditions for living than that offered by the barren and over-populated lands of the empire. After the conquest of these regions, the official work of colonization began on such a large scale that it resulted in the nearly total assimilation of the native population, which had resisted the isolated influence of the first pioneers of Roman civilization.

To realize how much Trajan wanted to colonize this new province, we should make reference to the text of the brilliant Roman historian Eutropius, who affirms that Trajan had transported to Dacia *infinitas copias bominum ad argos et urbes calendas.*

This fortunate province, which historians would call "Dacia Felix," was, unfortunately, in direct contact with both the Goths and the Slavs and, inevitably, destined to be invaded, and, consequently, to be abandoned by the Roman authorities, incapable of resisting forever the impetuous and continuous attacks of the barbarians. So, in the year 270, the Roman Emperor Aurelian, because of continuing pressure from the Goths, was compelled to abandon Dacia, withdrawing Roman troops and officials to Moesia, on the right bank of Danube.

This event is important because Magyar politicians and scholars use it today to justify their policies against the Romanian people.

The Hungarians quote in their favour incorrect information in the writings of the historians Eutropius and Flavius Vopiscus, who stated that Dacia was completely abandoned by its population. They use these statements to argue that at the time of the Hungarian invasion (895 A.D.) it was really uninhabited. According to their "theory," the Romanians, who later appeared on these lands, on the both sides of the Carpathians, are not the descendants of the ancient Dacians, but only some intruders who came to Pannonia from across the Danube during the Middle Ages:

> They arrived in this province [later to be called Transylvania] after it had already become a Hungarian land. Despite their superior numbers, they cannot ask for equal rights [with us] because we, the Magyars, are the sole owners of this land.[8]

---

[8]Rössler, *Rumänische Studien.* Leipzig, 1871. Hunvalphy, *Az olaho Törtenete.* Budapest, 1894; De Bertha, *Magyars et Roumains devant l'histoire.* Paris, 1899.

Because today the principle *"Prior tempore potior jure"* can no longer be used to justify the persecution of one segment of the population by another, we will demonstrate that the Magyars cannot use this so-called historical right.

The historical argument built by the Hungarians has a very fragile support; their logic is faulty, one of their most important premises being completely false.

Dacia was not uninhabited at the time of the Hungarian invasion and, if we should call anyone an "intruder" in Pannonia it certainly is not the Romanian people.

Of course, Aurelian's troops left Dacia, along with the civil servants and perhaps a large part of the upper classes of this colony, but it has been proven on many occasions, as we shall see later on, that most colonists — farmers, shepherds, and mine owners, with strong connections to the land, (bonds that exist even today) — did not leave their properties. They stayed here to defend them against the barbarians. They remained here to fulfill their great mission as Latin sentinels on the border of the Eastern World.[9]

Historical Evidence

1. The historian-monk Nestor, in the eleventh century, said that the Magyars encountered, at the time of their invasion in Pannonia, a very large Romanian population. This affirmation must be looked at alongside that of the Hungarian Thomas, who says that Transylvania *dicitur antiquitus fuisse pascua Romanorum.* Even the Hungarian historian Kéza admits that Pannonia was still inhabited by a Romanian population at the time of the Magyar invasion. The Romanian population included in that period "old shepherds and Roman colonists." Even a Greek historian, Nicétas Choniates, recorded their existence in Transylvania in the year 1100.

"The anonymous chronicler" of King Bela II, who wrote a history of the Hungarian settlement in Pannonia, talks in detail about the struggles between the Magyars and "the Romanian leaders" in Transylvania. Two of these leaders, Litovoi and Seneslau, ruled in 1247, the former ruled some

---

[9]Général Niox, *Les pays balkaniques.* Paris, Delagrave, 1915, p. 44; Cf. the great work of Julius Jung of the University of Prague, *Die Romanischen Landschaften des romischen Reiches,* Insbruck, 1881, pp. 314–381; *Römer und Romanen in Donauländer,* Insbruck, 1877, etc.

lands in the mountains of Little Wallachia and the latter in the mountains of Greater Wallachia. The existence of Litovoi's small country, belonging to the Basarabs, is also confirmed by the Persian chronicler Fazel-Ulach-Rachid, who describes their wars with the Tartars in 1241.[10]

The name of one such Romanian leader, Herzog Romunc, and those of his Wallachian comrades can be found also in a famous poem (*Nibelun-genlied*). The importance of this fact is even greater if we take into consideration the idea that this poem was written at the time of the invasion of the Huns five centuries before the arrival of the Magyars. It is very clear that the Romanians who did not leave Dacia organized them-selves, step by step, into independent principalities, each having their own organization, leaders, and even their own armies.

An important number of royal maps from the twelfth and thirteenth centuries, as well as many Greek chroniclers and a considerable number of Magyar and German texts confirm our thesis.

2. The toponomy of ancient Dacia has remained almost the same, especially in the mountain areas. This is additional evidence of the con-tinuity of the Romanian population. Rivers, mountains, and even towns have kept their ancient Roman, Dacian, or Scythian names, as Herodo-tus mentioned them. So, how can the Magyars explain this miraculous coincidence if, as they affirm, Dacia was totally abandoned by all its Dacian-Roman inhabitants? How did the Magyars find, on their own, six centuries later, those Latin, Dacian, or Scythian names that were used by the Roman colonists and by the native population to call their mountains, rivers, and colonies. For over 30 years Magyar historians have been look-ing for an answer to this question, but they have been unsuccessful.

3. In order to explain the existence of the Romanian population in Dacia alter the Roman withdrawal in 274 ordered by the Emperor Aure-lian, the Magyars plead for a Romanian remigration that took place (of course!) after their establishment in Pannonia. It is obvious that this sup-

---

[10]Here are some Hungarian sources that support our thesis:

"*Isti enim Zaculi Hunorum residui, qui dum Hungaros in Panoniam literatos cognoverunt, non tamen in plano Panoniac: sed enim Blachis in montibus confiniis sortem habuerunt unde Blachis comixti literis ipsorum uti perhibentur.*" Kéza, lib. I., cap.V, p. 6.

"*Tune habitatores (Blachi) terrae (ultra silvanae) videntes mortem domini sui (Blachi Gelu), sua propria voluntae dextram dantes dominum sibi eligerunt tuhutum, qui a die illo terram illiam obtinuit pacifice et feliciter.*" Anonimi Belac rcgis notarii, c. 27.

"*...ut nulum tributum debeant persolvere cum transierint per terram siculorum ant Blachoru, homines nunc quoque terram habitante.*" Diploma Andrei regis (1.221).

position cannot be verified in any documents, chronicles, legends, or traditions of this nation.

It is absolutely impossible for such an important event to have taken place at that time without leaving any kind of trace.

On the contrary, many documents and inscriptions from the thirteenth and fourteenth centuries bring us a new evidence to support our theory that Moldavia and Wallachia were found by leaders from the north (and not from the south), from Transylvania and Maramureş, and not from Moesia. Their capitals were towns located in the mountains, such as Câmpulung and Târgovişte, and not in the Danubian plain, as would have been logical if the Magyar theory had any basis at all. Many ethnographic, philological, and historical arguments contradict in the politically motivated and unscientific theory invented by Magyar historians to serve their cause.

The rhetoric of Rössler, Hunvalfy, and Bartha did not succeed in convincing anyone, not even serious Magyar scholars. In 1910, at the order of the Royal Magyar Trade Minister, the Art Institute of the Royal Court in Budapest published a beautiful work entitled *Hungary*, a collaborative work to which many important Magyar scholars contributed: Dr. Julius Bondar, Stephen Barsony, Dr. Samuel Borovszky, Dr. Béla Erödi, Béla Gonda, Dr. Guillaume Hankô, Dr. Luis Locsy, Th. Nôvak, Dr. Wilibald Semayer, Carol Siegmeth, Dr. Jan Szyklay, Dr. Ladislas Toldy, etc. In this work (on page 13), we find a very important declaration:

> The tools of the troops of the Roman emperors brought our state beside the other civilized states and that is why we cannot admit that after Pannonia's loss the warriors from different nations who were settled there and who had gathered, through their own work, lands, vineyards, and houses, left behind, together with their families, everything that they owned and departed from Dacia to look for a new country. *Ubi bene, ibi patria*: this line echoes all too true when it is pronounced by the first civilized human beings.

We agree with them completely.

Consequently, the Magyars cannot justify their immoral claims, not even with the help of the so-called "historical right" that serves as a basis to support their sad political system of violence and oppression.

Having clarified this problem, we should next examine the political situation of the Romanians over the centuries. In Middle Ages, the Romanians were divided into three different political groups: on one side of the

Carpathians, Moldavia[11] and Wallachia, both principalities, and the great principality of Transylvania on the other side.

In the fifteenth century, too powerless to resist any longer the violent attacks of their neighbors, the Romanians of Moldavia and Wallachia were forced to go to Constantinople to ask the Ottoman emperor for help. According to Romanian leaders, this was the only way to maintain the autonomy of their principalities.

In this way, under the Ottoman hegemony, the Romanian principalities maintained their complete autonomy. Only the trans-Carpathian principality was occupied by the Magyars; but it kept its own separate political autonomy, organization, institutions, council (Diet), and leaders. It had only a very weak feudal connection with Hungary, but this still existed.[12]

After the battle of Mohács in 1526, Transylvania succeeded in freeing itself from Hungarian domination and in becoming an independent principality with its own leaders.

In 1599 the three Romanian principalities — Transylvania, Moldavia, and Wallachia — were united by the great Wallachian ruler Prince Michael the Brave. This historical event lasted only a brief moment, but its memory remained fresh in the minds of the Romanians for centuries thereafter. The assassination of the great leader by General Basta, with the consent of Hungarian leaders, ended the Romanians' brief and sweet dream. After Michael the Brave's assassination, Transylvania still maintained its independence, so that in the Treaty of Westphalia (1648) it was counted among the independent states of Europe.

Weakened by its endless struggles against the Ottomans on the one hand and the Hungarian and Polish armies on the other, Transylvania was forced to ask for outside help. The Austrian emperor offered his help and Transylvania entered into an alliance with the House of Hapsburg, represented by Leopold I.

This date (1691) was one of the most important moments in the history of the principality, because this was the moment when the relationship between Transylvania and Austria was sealed forever by a famous document, *Diploma Leopoldinum*. This public contract accepted by Leopold I and also by the Transylvanian Diet is the principal document on

---

[11] Up to the eighteenth century Moldavia included Bucovina and Bessarabia.

[12] Brorc, *Chestiunea română in Transilvania și Ungaria.* Bucharest, Voința Națională, 1895, p. 14 ff.; Henry Gaidoz, *Les Roumains de Hongrie.* Paris, Chaix, 1894, p. 11; Popovici, *La question roumaine de Transylvanie.* Vienna, 1892, p. 9 ff. and also quoted on pp. 45, 46.

the basis of which Transylvania was governed up to 1867. According to this document, Transylvania's autonomy was forever recognized, with all its rights: the right of governing by its own laws, the right to make laws only by its own Diet, the right of having its own financial system, the right of electing its own statesmen. This Diploma was recognized and confirmed, without any objection, by all the emperors who succeeded Leopold I.

Under Emperor Charles VI, the pragmatic approval (changing the order of succession to the throne of Austria) was recognized in 1722 by the Transylvanian Diet, which did not neglect the opportunity to remind the emperor, once more, of the principality's autonomy and independence from Hungary.

In 1790, during the reign of Joseph II, the Diet once again acclaimed its autonomy, in a way that disturbed the emperor who had intentions of limiting its independence. The Diet firmly declared that *per se subsitens et ab alio regno independents principatus Transilvaniae.*

Leopold II (1791) and his successor Ferdinand I (1837) again confirmed the principality's autonomy.

Emperor Franz Joseph did exactly the same thing as his predecessors and recognized it in a document sent to the Transylvanian Diet on 15 June 1863. On 21 August of the same year, the Diet, having doubts about the sincerity and the intentions of this ruler, answered this imperial message with a convincing memorial reminding the sovereign which were their rights and privileges. It emphasizes "the independence and integrity of this great principality preserved throughout the centuries;" it also reminds us that, on 4 December 1691, Emperor Leopold I only took Transylvania under his protection and that the document from 1691 was "a public one, made in a very serious manner, that could not be annulled."

The emperor answered this memorial on 5 September 1863 to demonstrate to them his loyal feelings and to admit the civic and juridical importance of this document, forever memorable.

Consequently, Transylvania's autonomy was recognized in a very clear manner, once more, by the same person who, a few years later, gave it to the Magyars.

This historical event deserves our attention because it is the moral, juridical, and historical basis for the claims of all the nations of Transylvania.

Defeated in 1866 at Sadova, Austria was forced to make peace with the Magyars, whom, up to that time, it had kept under its domination only through a harsh policy of repression. Hungary claimed as the price for reconciliation its complete independence, the recognition of equal rights with the Austrians, and the right to annex Transylvania. At that moment, Franz Joseph, in order to save the dynasty, forgetting his promises to the Transylvanian Diet, forgetting the services of "his loyal and brave Romanian nation"[13] against the Magyars, agreed to the immoral act called "the compromise (*Ausgleich*) of 1867" which abolished Transylvania's autonomy.[14]

According to this, the great Principality of Transylvania became Hungarian property and lost all its rights; "the name of Transylvania is from now on nothing but a geographical expression."[15]

From this moment on, the Hungarian nation became the master of this principality and its sole purpose was the transformation of the Romanian population in the province into "Magyars."

As we shall see, they quickly set to work.

* * *

Bucovina's history is much simpler. Being a part of Moldavia it was the political center of the principality, of the metropolitan bishops, already from the founding of the principality in the fourteenth century. It never ceased to be a part of Moldavia, Suceava being for many centuries its capital.

In 1775 the Ottoman Empire, which, as we have shown, was only the suzerain over Moldavia and Wallachia, ceded Bucovina to Austria

---

[13]In 1848 Franz Joseph sent the following message to the Romanians: "I am glad to accept the homage of the loyal and brave Romanian nation and I recognize its great sacrifices made for my throne and the unity of the monarchy against an unscrupulous party which is responsible for the present civil war." In 1848 the Romanians formed "a loyal and brave nation" while the Magyars were only a party but, after 1867, the Magyars became in the emperor's eyes "a noble nation" while the Romanians became "an unscrupulous party."

[14]The Hungarians, who had planned for a long time this annexation, influenced the voting in the Diets of 1848 and 1865 to favor the annexation of Transylvania by Hungary. These councils, from which the Romanians were excluded, did not represent the wishes of the Transylvanian population of which the Romanians were the preponderant nation. (See Lavisse and Rambaud, *Histoire générale*. Paris, Collin, 1899, XI, p. 121; Popovici, *op. cit.* p. 33; B. Auerbach, *Les races et les nationalités d'Autriche-Hongrie*. Paris, Alcan, 1917, p. 406, etc.)

[15]Lavisse and Rambaud, *op. cit.*, XI, p. 175.

despite the opposition of the prince of Moldavia who paid for his refusal to accept this injustice with his life.

But this act was illegal, both from a juridical, historical, and political point of view.

The Ottoman Empire could not cede to Austria a territory that did not belong to it because, as we have previously affirmed, Moldavia and Wallachia were never part of the Ottoman Empire. The sultan in Constantinople was only the suzerain of these principalities, which had their own leaders, laws, institutions, finances, and even their own armies. All the treaties between the Ottomans and the principalities guaranteed, without any exceptions, their territorial integrity.

The juridical principle *Nemo plus jure transfere potest quam ipse habe-ret* received its full application in this case.

This act of injustice, in violation of international laws and treaties, is invalid not only for historical reasons, but also for serious political reasons, because the Romanians form the majority of the population of this province, and have preserved their nationality and never stopped to demand the reintegration of this Romanian province where it rightfully belongs.[16]

It would be useless to insist further on the demands of Romania concerning this province.

Ethnographic Evidence

The ethnographic map of Hungary, after Auerbach, presents the image of a battlefield, with the Magyars in the center being surrounded on all sides by the Romanians, Serbians, Croats, Slovaks, Ruthenians, etc.

The Magyars are fewer in number than the Romanians or the Slavs. According to the latest census (1910) in Hungary, the nationalities are distributed as follows:

	million	%
Magyars	10.050	48.2
Romanians	2.950	14.1
Germans	2.030	9.8

[16]According to Austrian statistics, it is true that the Ruthenians also form a large community; but it is necessary to remember that these statistics are never concerned with the inhabitants' nationality, but only with their use of language (*Umgagssprache*) and the Romanians adopted the Ruthenian language in some regions for everyday activities. (See Simiginovirz. *Die Volkergruppen der Bukovina*. Czernovitz, Pardini, 1885, quoted by Auerbach, p. 268.)

Slovaks	1.960	9.4
Croats	1.830	8.8
Serbians	1.110	5.3
Ruthenians	0.470	2.3
Others	0.460	2.1

Even though the royal statistics were made in such a way so that everyone would believe that the nationalities problem in Hungary is less important than it appears, that the Magyars form the majority, and that the process of Magyarization is proceeding well, we will use official statistics. We do this with pleasure because, even using these official statistics, our thesis is undeniable.

First of all it is necessary to present the strange process of gathering information, unique in all of Europe, used by the Hungarian authorities.

The investigations never indicate the nationality of those who were questioned. In a procedure destined to establish the nationality of the inhabitants, they were, in fact, never asked about their nationality. They did not have to say if they were Romanians, Magyars, or Serbs, instead they had to specify their language. It is easy to understand why the results were wrong.

"Why do they avoid an honest and direct investigation concerning their nationalities? Why there isn't there a special item for this notion which is key to the basis of political and social life in Austria and Hungary?" wondered Auerbach, somewhat naively.[17]

To the question "Which language do you use?" Dr. Cantacuzino explained:

A great number of Romanians, especially those who worked in the public or private administration (civil servants, priests, etc.), under the pressure of intimidation, answered that their "preferred" language was Hungarian. In the final statistics, the favored language became "the native language" and those who answered in this way found themselves registered as Magyars. Using this same method, infants, mutes, Gypsies or the Roma, who formed large communities in Hungary, were also registered as Magyars.

The answer is simple: because true statistics would reveal the scope of Magyar policy and that their claims have no basis. These unfair statistics should open peoples' minds and should prove to the

---

[17] B. Auerbach, *Les races et les nationalités en Autriche-Hongrie*. Paris, Alcan, 1917, p. 22.

nationalities that they should become everything instead of being nothing.

In this very simple way, thousands and thousands of citizens were registered as being Magyars.[18]

These are the methods Professor Julius Jung criticized, calling the Hungarians "statistics falsifiers,"[19] while deputy Kramartz exposed them before the rostrum of the imperial council, classifying the entire system as "detestable cheating" (*Schwindel*).[20]

In other words, it is easy to prove that for the most part these statistics are false. Further on, we will provide some concrete examples.

According to official Hungarian statistics from 1890,[21] 17,349,398 inhabitants formed the population of Hungary, of which 7,426,730 were Magyars and 9,922,668 (57.80%) were of other nationalities; of these 2,591,900 were Romanians. So, according to the numbers from 1850 to 1890, the Magyar population would have increased, in a very unusual manner, by 35.74%, while that of other nationalities did not increase by more than 6.23%. The number of Romanians during this period would have declined from 2,648,000 to 2,591,905. These numbers conflict sharply with statistics which indicated that the Romanian population was the most prolific one in the empire.[22]

We also cite the case of the county of Turocz (Târnave) where the number of Magyars increased between 1900 and 1910 by 154%; in Zolyoni (Zalău) the increase was 82% and in Lipto 60%.[23]

Even if all these false statistics sought to hide the truth, the Magyar authorities did not succeed in proving the impossible. These remarkable "works of art" have proven nothing but their lack of objectivity and their nationalist extremism.[24]

---

[18] *La Revue hebdomadaire*, 20 March 1915.

[19] *Romer und Romanen in den Donaulandern*. Insbruck, Wagner, 1877, p. 300.

[20] The meeting of 24 November 1909, see Auerbach, p. 22.

[21] *A magyar Korona országainak helysegnévtára. Dr. jekelfalussy Joszef. Kiadja a.m.k. statisztikai hivatal.* Budapest, 1892.

[22] *The Statistical Yearbook*, XIX, 1911, p. 42, chart 20, see Auerbach, p. 344.

[23] Ibid., p. 344.

[24] Concerning "the scientific value of these statistics" we used the evidence of Naumann, *Mitteleuropa*, Berlin, 1915, p. 88 ff.

According to official Hungarian statistics from 1910, the population was as follows:

	Romanians	Hungarians	Germans	Slovaks	Serbians	Other
Transylvania	1,472,024	918,217	234,085	2,404	421	11,219
Banat	592,049	242,152	387,545	22,131	284,329	53,927
Crişana	654,281	581,162	43,416	25,537	2,517	10,000
Maramureş	213,863	322,805	66,949	928	34	162,087
Total	2,933,214	2,064,336	731,995	51,000	287,301	277,301
%	46.2%	32.5%	11%	0.8%	4.5%	4.1%

We have the possibility, at least partially, to correct these absolutely false numbers thanks to the statistics, also official, concerning religious denominations.

These statistics present the number of people in Hungary belonging to the "Uniate" and "Eastern-Greek" denominations. Those who belong to these churches are the Romanians, the Ruthenians, and some Slovaks.

From the total number of believers, dividing those of the non-Romanian nationalities, the following numbers resulted[25] concerning the nationalities in Transylvania as reflected in the following graph:

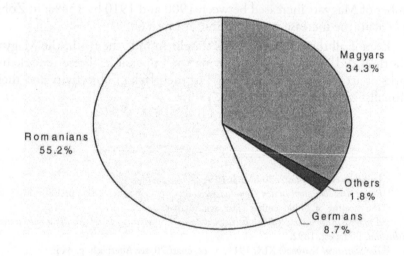

Magyars 34.3%

Romanians 55.2%

Others 1.8%

Germans 8.7%

---

[25] Şirianu, *op.cit*; Brote, *op.cit.*, p. 414;

According to Dr. Weigand, the larger percentage of the Ruthenian population compared to that of the Romanians could be attributed to the capacity for adaptation of the Romanian element, which he considered "more plastic, more polyglot" and which easily adopted the Ruthenian language.[26]

The author of this work, after a study journey made in 1906 in Bucovina, realized that the official statistics did not reflect the reality at all, the real number of the Romanian population being much greater than that of the other peoples mentioned in the statistical data.

These differences surprised us especially in Suceava, Sucevița, Gura Humorului, Voroneț, Rădăuți, Câmpulung, Vatra Dornei, Putna, etc.

Even if we inverted the percentages of the Romanians and the Ruthenians, the numbers would not correspond to reality because the actual number of Romanians in this area is over 350,000.

According to the both Hungarian and Austrian statistics, the total number of Romanians in the above-mentioned provinces is approximately 3,205,468 persons.

Correcting these numbers, as we have already done, results in a final number of 3,473,335 Romanians. If we take into consideration the manner in which the census was conducted and the spirit in which it took place, we can fairly say that their actual number is probably over 4,000,000.

To illustrate the grouping of these Romanian elements, we should take a look at an ethnographic and political map elaborated according to the data from the official statistics:

> We see, in the heart of Transylvania, a small Magyar island surrounded and crossed by the smaller islands, of Germans, the whole being "drowned out" by a wide mass of Romanians. Then, as we approach the outskirts of the Romanian region, to the east and to the north, we notice that the Romanian groups are growing rarer again, or are penetrated by foreign elements. So, the whole territory is surrounded by a mixed area, in which, even with the large presence of the Romanians, the foreign elements are still dominating: the Serbians and the Germans to the eastern border of Banat, in the angle made by the confluence of Tisa with the Danube River; the Magyars in the Crișana area, close to the Tisa River; the Ruthenians in the northern parts of both Maramureș and Bucovina.

---

[26]See Auerbach, *op. cit.*

In Maramureş, the superior course of river Tisa forms a natural border between the Romanian and Ruthenian areas; Bucovina, with its capital city at Cernăuţi, is situated at the limit of two territories.

Taking a look at such a map, we can make only a terse impression and not in the least in accordance with reality; for example, in some parts of Transylvania designated as belonging to the Hungarians, the Magyar population in not homogeneous at all and is mixed with many Romanian elements; the same situation exists also in the German areas.

The statistics show us that in almost every county, even those in which the foreign elements are deeply infiltrated, the inhabitants of Romanian nationality are in a considerable proportion.

Thus, in Transylvania, in the 81 administrative districts which form the whole province, there are:

in	14	administrative districts	90.95%	Romanians
in	16	administrative districts	80.90%	Romanians
in	8	administrative districts	70.80%	Romanians
in	20	administrative districts	50.70%	Romanians
in	7	administrative districts	40.50%	Romanians
in	3	administrative districts	30.40%	Romanians
in	2	administrative districts	15.30%	Romanians
in	10	administrative districts	2.15%	Romanians
in	1	administrative district	- %	Romanians

(Data presented by Dr. I. Cantacuzino in *Revista Săptămânală*, no. 12, 20 March 1915)

Consequently, the Romanians represent an absolute majority in 71% of the administrative districts and are missing altogether in only one district.

Again, we repeat that these official statistics are much lower than the real numbers.

Our thesis, at least from this point of view, is not contested even by the Magyars, who admit the prevalence of the Romanian element in these regions.

Thus, in the official work *Ungaria*, previously quoted, we find (p. 333) this declaration: "the main mass of the population of Transylvania is presently formed by the Romanians"; and on p. 11 the following precious findings:

The northwestern part of Upper Hungary is inhabited by almost two million Slovaks, while 400,000 Ruthenians are living in the north-eastern Carpathians' valleys. The region surrounded by the elevations of the Transylvanian mountains is inhabited by almost three million Romanians.

If these are the statements of the Hungarian authorities, we can easily imagine what the real situation is like.

The Policy of "Magyarization" in the Romanian Provinces in Hungary

Now, let us see how the 4,000,000 Romanians are treated by the Austro-Hungarian minority; what are their rights in their own lands, after the establishment of the regime of compromise in 1867.

In order not to be suspected of being partial, we use information provided by German historians about whom our opponents cannot think badly.

We will then call on French and English writers who have let the civilized world know about Hungarian actions long before 1914, at a time when the Hungarians were considered both in Paris and London as "the classic lovers of liberty." As such, these testimonies cannot be suspected of partiality.

We will start with the Germans:

The historian Fessler, who has studied the problem first-hand, declared that "these Romanians, who once were the masters of Transylvania and who, even today, form the crushing majority of the population, have been subdued by other nations and are increasingly in the situation of slavery."[27]

Another historian, Leopold von Ranke, who characterized the Hungarian policies concerning the Romanians as being "hateful and reactionary," made the same finding.[28]

A French scholar, Leroy Beaulieu, who knew very well the Hungarian political problems, wrote the following lines over 23 years ago,[29] at a moment when the Hungarians enjoyed all the support of France:

> I am one of those who were, along the Hungarians, happy with their victory over Austro-German centralism. That is why it is so

---

[27] *Geschichte von Ungaru.* Leipzig, 1885, vol. V, p. 547.

[28] *Weltgeschichte.* Leipzig, Drucher und Humboldt, 1883, pp. 111, 272, zur rumanisch-magyarischen Streitfrage, p. 448 ff. Wien, Walshauer, 1891.

[29] *Voix latines*, Bucharest, Sacec, 1894, p. 26

hard for me to forgive their lack of generosity toward the other nationalities of the crown of Saint Stephen. I am convinced that they are wrong, that sooner or later the Hungarians will pay for their oppressive policies toward the nations that, in the end, are by no means inferior to the descendants of Arpad.

Henri Rochefort denounced "the Hungarian oppression and persecution of the Romanians, who are being treated like wild animals in Transylvania..." and wonders:

How come such infamies are still possible in our time? Why have the European powers not constituted themselves up to now as a great court of arbitration, authorized to stop the oppression of one nation by another. We could say that we have not evolved much since the stone age.[30]

Georges Clémenceau, an expert in the problem of the nationalities of Hungary, after having recounted the history of the "legitimate" Romanian claims, rises with the same energy against "this sovereignty of force raised to the principle of public right in Transylvania by the Hungarians" and then adds: "...the Romanians have only Justice on their side. This is an insignificant word, but the Hungarians knew how to make it important. This, like their history, should be a lesson to us."[31]

Juliette Adam wrote the following lines in the *Nouvelle Revue* on 15 May 1894:

The Hungarian liberals, if being analyzed from the point of view of Vienna's politics, are just like the Austrian and German liberals, authoritative: liberals only in matters concerning their own groups, party, and politics.

Without taking into consideration their egalitarian traditions, for they are the sons of the 1848 Revolution, they oppress the non-Hungarian nationalities, as much as the Austrian Empire had previously oppressed the Hungarians.

It is known what happens, despite Kossuth's promises of emancipation, even despite the same promises by Déak concerning the small Slav nationalities in the realm of Saint Stephen. For more than forty years this situation has been going on in Transylvania, which the successors of the Germanophile Tisza are obstinate to make Hungarian; but the Romanians living in Transylvania and Banat are conscious of their ethnic affiliation and prefer to remain Latins.

---

[30] Ibid., p. 38
[31] Ibid., pp. 105–107

The discriminatory laws that govern Transylvania are a continuing threat. Four million Romanians live under the regime of a government that guarantees exceptional favors only for the Germans.

Flourens, former minister of France, wrote the following in 1894:

It would be an imprudence on our part to allow to be crushed, under the power of the oppression of the Germans and the Hungarians, a Romanian population of ten million which has constituted throughout the centuries a vanguard of Latin civilization toward the Orient, which, when the nationalities will group together scientifically by their affinities of nation, origin, and language, will necessarily grow closer to the Latin nations and will assume for them the role of an advanced sentinel...

At the beginning of this century, the Hungarians knew how to conquer public opinion throughout liberal Europe, through boldness, courage, and perseverance to achieve their national claims. As their struggles against the titanic oppression of Austria and the backward thinking Viennese bureaucracy took a long time, France did not withhold encouragement or appreciation...

Today, barely relieved of German despotism, they assist their German allies in making life even more burdensome for those who, until recently, were their companions in grief, battle, and misfortune, and they also gradually lose the sympathy of those who gave them strength and helped them to triumph.

The free nations of Western Europe defended the cause of the Hungarians against the German oppressors when the old German despotism denied their equality in rights. They must not be surprised if the attitude of the same nations turns against them, when, in their blind and tyrannical chauvinism, they deny not only civil and political equality, but also the right to exist to the Slavs and Romanians, who are only tied together by a geography recently invented for the needs of the uncertain equilibrium of an illegitimate political system in Transylvania.

The claims of the Romanians, coexisting in equal number, if not more numerous than the Hungarians, on the land of Transylvania, are most just and moderate and they impress you, by reading them, that, at the end of the nineteenth century, a European nation was brought in a state of having to demand the exertion of rights so essential and so undeniable.[32]

---

[32] *Voix latines*, p. 109.

A well-known Englishman, R.W. Seton-Watson, who writes under the pseudonym of Scotus Viator, after having completed a long and thorough first-hand research about the issues that interest us, published in 1905 and 1908 two works named *The Future of Austria-Hungary*[33] and *La persécution politique en Hongrie.*[34]

The Hungarian newspaper *As Ujsag* from Budapest expressed itself enthusiastically about this writer: "He knows so well our greatest problems, he appreciates them so precisely that instead of having to teach this foreign writer, we can learn something from him."

The *Berliner Tageblatt* declared that "Scotus Viator is a man that sees the situation in Europe through the eyes of an expert, with clear judgement, and he especially discerns the complicated situation in the Orient."

The newspapers *Neue Freie Presse* and *Die Zeit* in Vienna, *Allgemeine Zeitung* in Munich, and *Kölnische Zeitung* in Köln have all praised this man whose works are true indictments of "the barbarous behavior" of the Hungarians who, because of their policies toward the nationalities, "have lost their right to be called civilized." These works of incontestable impartiality will help us throughout this brief study, to provide accurate examples.

Henry Wickam Steed, who lived there for ten years and confessed an undeniable sympathy for the Hungarian monarchy, was still forced to write the following lines:

> The Hungarians do not see anything that does not conform to their wishes; when it comes to things opposed to their wishes they become blind. The Hungarians have practiced very few times the virtue of temperance. By forgetting that the arrangement in 1867 represented a maximum that could have been pulled out of the dynasty under the pressure of the circumstances, they have insistently favored a Hungarian chauvinism, extremely violent spirit; and with Koloman Tisza as prime minister of Hungary between 1875 and 1890, this chauvinism became state policy.[35]

Although risking the loyalty of important nations like Romanians in Transylvania, Emperor Franz Joseph tolerated the tactics of Tisza and the Hungarian prime ministers who succeeded him; he showed

---

[33] London, Constable et Co., 1905
[34] French translation. Paris. Ed. Cornely, 1908.
[35] *La monarchie des Habsburg.* Paris, A. Colin, 1916, p. 66

himself to be indifferent to the use of corruption and oppression as a means to govern.[36]

As in the problem of the South Slavs, in this matter Hungarian chauvinism must be condemned. By trying in vain to make Hungarians a prolific and by no means intellectually inferior nation, the Hungarians have destroyed the feeling of loyalty the Romanians had toward the Hungarian state and their dynasty and have endangered the Austro-Hungarian system of resistance against Russia in Southeastern Europe.[37]

It is twenty years since Lavisse and Rambaud, in their considerable *Histoire générale*, condemned this policy of transforming other nations into Hungarians and declared themselves against the measures taken in Transylvania "with unparalleled rigor and meanness."[38]

By chance we came across an article published in *Gazette de Lausanne* on 11 September 1914 which seemed interesting because it contained testimonies from an impartial Swiss visitor in Transylvania:

These people take water out with their bare hands to water their melons. These melons are their obsession: this is the base of their nourishment, along with some corn. The Romanians eat almost nothing; they are satisfied if they are paid with barely a franc a day. Excellent farmers, they know nothing but the ancient plow. The Hungarians are afraid that the Romanians might become wealthy. For being wealthy might allow them to buy a piece of land and in this way obtain the right to vote.

The Hungarian regime is abominable; *populus et plebs*, aristocracy and *nuisera plebs contribuens* are the terms that have remained through time since the Hungarian constitution in the thirteenth century. Which is an anachronism for the twentieth century.

Tsingare, beggars, Romanians that kiss hands, Hungarians in fancy clothes and braids; and in the background the supervision of the police and the gun of the tax collector; this is all you see in today's Transylvania. Watermelons and flour for the Romanians, wines and paprika-flavored food for the Hungarians, and not a drop of wheat where a free nation could harvest thousands!

---

[36] Ibid., p. 69.
[37] Ibid., p. 420.
[38] Lavisse and Rambaud, *op. cit.*, Volume XII, p. 170.

We could go on quoting many other testimonies by French, English, Italian, and even German tourists, whose hearts went out to the Romanians when seeing their miserable situation.

For the Romanians in this province there are no rights, no freedom, and no honor.

They are at the discretion of the Hungarian gendarmes. They are forbidden to leave their fields, all progress has been taken away from them, they are forbidden to study and express their thoughts, meet their fellow countrymen, speak their own language, and, recently, they were forbidden to pray according to their religion.

A merciless campaign to destroy their nation has been going on for fifty years directed against everything that is Romanian, with a violence and arrogance unheard of among other nations in Europe.

It was not in vain that Bismarck, who knew people, and the Hungarians in particular, called the Magyars "the most arrogant nation in Europe."

* * *

The Magyar persecutions against the Romanians can be classified into five groups and, for the reader's enlightenment, we will examine each of them.

Electoral persecutions. Trying to make the parliament inaccessible to the Romanians, to keep them out of public life and thus to deprive them of any possibility to defend publicly their rights and interests, the Magyars adopted, since 1876, an exceptional electoral law. This law, applied only in the regions inhabited by Romanians, imposed a poll tax four to eight times higher than that imposed on people in the rest of Hungary and this when there were many exemptions from these taxes for other parts of the population. In 1914, Count Tisza, who was then Hungary's prime minister, being convinced of the righteousness of this law and the fact that it satisfied the chauvinism of his powerful party, succeeded in adopting another law, even more oppressive, according to which the only citizens who were entitled to vote were those who were "educated." To obtain the right to vote, they had to prove before a committee that they knew how to write and read. This committee, formed exclusively of government agents, rejected without mercy the Romanians, claiming that they were not well-enough educated, while they proved to be more than indulgent with the Magyars.

The way in which the electoral lists are prepared throws light upon the local administration in Hungary.

Some of the electors' name were omitted by chance or wrongly spelled or there were mistakes concerning their age or profession and in this way they were disqualified. All the documents were written in Magyar and the smallest mistakes in this language served as a pretext for excluding them. The votes were sometimes annulled for the strangest reasons.

Even in these extreme cases, these votes were considered to be for the opposition candidate.[39]

But even with all this the Magyar government in Budapest doubted the effectiveness of their policies. As a result, the government changed the boundaries of the electoral districts to make them more favorable to the Magyars and more unfavorable to the Romanians. So, despite the preponderance of the Romanian population in Transylvania which was divided into 370 electoral districts, there were only 50 in which the Romanians formed the majority.

But at least, if they had the right to vote for whoever they wanted.

But the supreme count, tells us a Transylvanian citizen, the viscount, the priests, the mayors, the policemen were almost exclusively Magyars sent into Transylvania by the Hungarian government.[40]

By election day these Magyar representatives had done their best to influence the election results.

All these public figures, who did not actually have the right to influence this result, decided and determined the results of the Magyar candidates.

These statements were sustained by the findings of other writers, including an English writer, Robert Seton-Watson, and a French visitor to Hungary, André Duboscq.

In his remarkable book *La Hongrie d'hier et d'aujourd'hui*,[41] the latter writes:

There, the vote is oral, which leads us to believe that the vote of those who need some favors cannot be a very sincere one. Even more, the voters who supported the opposition candidates could

---

[39]Scotus Viator, *op. cit.*, pp. 26, 30.

[40]Popovici, *op. cit.*, p. 18.

[41]Paris, Bloud, p. 9.

have many troubles, the smallest of which would be that their vote would not to be taken into consideration if they pronounced their candidate's name wrong. When they came in groups as they used to, the soldiers surrounded them to keep them far away from the registers; the name of the candidate was said twice, but the electors could not reach the registers because the soldiers blocked them and in this way the voting process was ended.

Seton-Watson's findings were exactly the same:

Not only were the electoral commissions corrupt, but even the civil servants were interfering in politics and participated in the electoral campaign without there existing any punishment for their breaking the law.[42]

To understand better the electoral procedures in Hungary, we should not forget that their law said that the vote should be taken publicly under the threatening eyes of the authorities.

Seton-Watson provides a series of examples concerning the "correctness of the Hungarian elections:"

On election day, some bridges were declared dangerous, so that the population had to walk miles and miles or to give up voting. Many electors were practically stopped by the army to get to the voting place.

If a group of peasants dared to do otherwise than the soldiers said, they were practically shot. There was a case when twenty people were killed at a voting place.

Other times, in a Slovakian or Romanian district the authorities sent 1,000 soldiers and 300 gendarmes to "keep order;" the Magyar press is full of stories that present the acts of terrorism committed by the non-Magyar inhabitants.

The "correctness" of these elections is recounted in a story from the time of the elections in 1905 published in the *Pester Lloyd* newspaper:

"Cséke (Bihor). — The Romanian candidate influenced the Romanian population, so that he was arrested at the order of the *foszolgabiro* [a kind of deputy mayor]."[43]

---

[42]Scotus Viator, *op. cit.*, p. 31.
[43]Ibidem, p. 27.

An election in Transylvania is a real civil war in which the unarmed Romanian peasants have to obey the Hungarian army that would use their weapons any time.[44]

Despite all the stories previously mentioned, Seton-Watson believed that cases of violence rarely happened, but unfortunately this was not the case.

The Magyar newspapers mentioned many times similar cases and, despite their chauvinism, they considered that it was their duty to publicize them.

The Magyar newspaper *Egyetertés* gives its readers "an example of the fair way" in which the elections in Transylvania were conducted.

(At Turda)… The gendarmes forced the peasants to leave their houses. The Hungarian soldiers ran through the village gathering up people and forced them to go vote.[45]

Aurel Popovici describes the Chiosti case (Transylvania) that ended in the way Seton-Watson presented:

The Romanians, refusing to vote for the Magyar candidate, were brought by force to the voting place. Many of them were killed and wounded.[46]

Dr. Cantacuzino presents us with a list of similar cases:

26 April 1903 at Sereuş — The gendarmes, at the praetor's order, who came to assist in the regional elections, started to fire on the peasants who did not want to vote for his candidate. — Five dead and many wounded.

3/16 February 1905, at Cehul Silvaniei — The president of the electoral commission refused to watch out for the safety of the Romanians electors.

In front of the gendarmes, the Magyars hit George Pop de Băseşti, the president of the National Party who was 70 years old, over the head and wounded 30 other Romanian citizens; the president ordered that the victims should be arrested.

---

[44]M.R. Şirianu, *op. cit.* Cf.: H. Gaidoz, *Les Roumains de Hongrie.* Paris, Chaix, 1894, p. 21; L. Saintupery, *L'Europe politique, l'Autriche-Hongrie.* Paris, Lecéne, Oudin, 1893, p. 270.
[45]No. 30 from 1892.
[46]Popovici, *op. cit.*, p. 41.

Between 25 and 27 April 1906 at Amati, the Hungarians killed the friends of the nationalist candidate: G. Coraci, Ion Suta, and Iosif Dragoş.

Between 17 and 30 April 1906 at Bichiş, the gendarmes shot at the electors even before they voted. One dead and one wounded.

26 April 1906 at Cornia, soldiers killed Nicolae Pop, the son of Costa and also killed Ioan Glut, wounded Zaharia Pop, Costa Bert, and Ion Costin who wanted to go to the polls and vote for the Romanian candidate, Dr. Vaida (Şomcuta Mare).

29 April 1906 at Cehul Silvaniei the Magyars beat in a very cruel way priest Dumitru Pop from Moţ and Iacob Botis from Naprad. No one was punished.

9 May 1906 at Baia Mare. The Hungarians attacked, in the middle of the night, the Romanians electors at their own homes in order to force them not to vote in the elections. Six Romanians were killed and another three were seriously wounded. Finally, this time 27 Hungarians were arrested, but they were later found not guilty.

7 December 1910 at Galatt (Făgăraş). The peasants did not want to elect as their mayor the Hungarian priest's candidate, Distrai; they brought forward their own candidate and asked the authorities to recognize him. Distrai took it as a revolt and asked the soldiers to shoot. Three people were killed and another nine wounded.

In 1911 at Drama the gendarmes beat and stabbed one of the peasants, Grora.

In 1911 at Şoroc they beat the nationalist priest Romul Vasianu.

In 1911 at Făget (Banat) the Romanian Traian Murărescu was stabbed with bayonets.

In 1911 at Bomoş (Orăştic) they shot Mihai Hudiţă.

In 1912 and 1913 at Jelna (Alba Iulia) they shot and wounded many persons accused of demonstrations against Hungary because they did not want to give up their Romanian tricolor belt.[47]

This is the meaning of the "parliamentary regime" and "electoral correctness" in Hungary.

All this fraud and violence is acknowledged by those who took part in these charades that were called "legislative elections." Because of these practices, the Romanians, who should have had at least 75 places in the House of Deputies in Budapest, had only 5 of 516.[48]

---

[47] See Dr. Cantacuzino's article in *Revue hebdomaire*.
[48] See the *Jurnal de Genéve* newspaper of 1 June 1917.

The situation of the Serbs, the Slovaks, and the Slovenians was similar to that of the Romanians, perhaps with some exceptions in their account.

The suppression of the Romanian language. The Romanian language was no longer used in public schools, public administration, courts, and even in Romanian churches.

Even if they had the same obligations as the Magyars, the Romanians did not have even one public school where their children could learn in their own language as the fundamental law of 1868, called "the nationalities law," promised.

Despite the great number of protests by the Romanian nationalists to obtain the rights promised by the law of 1868, this law was completely annulled.[49]

In this way the Romanians were forced, using their own money, to build their own private schools where the Romanian language was taught.

Up to 1905 the Romanians built over 3,500 primary schools. This led the Hungarians to adopt punitive measures. Even if the Romanian language was the main one in these schools, the Magyar language was not forgotten. Each week there were several classes in which this language was studied.

Even more, Count Apponyi (the Hungarian minister of Public Education) adopted new laws in 1907 that said that the Hungarian authorities had the right to close Romanian schools where the Magyar language was superficially treated. Every year, more and more schools were closed for this reason.

---

[49]On the basis of article 44 of this law, lawyers had the possibility to plead their causes, in most cases, in their maternal language (points 3 and 7). The employees of the courts are compelled to use the language of the nationalities (point 6); religious communities have the right to choose the language for their registers, in schools, and for their service (point 14 ff.).

Also, the Ministry of Public Instruction will supervise that in state-administered schools instruction shall be made in the maternal language of the citizens, if they are in a sufficiently large number for each region, this up to the level of higher education (point 17). Point 18 stipulates that for regions where several languages are spoken, a department for the language and literature of each of these languages will be constituted. The employees of the communes are compelled to use, in their relationships with the inhabitants of the respective commune, the native language of the latter (point 21). Finally, point 27 stipulates the principle that the citizens' nationality will not represent an obstacle in being appointed to public offices. We will soon see how this law was enforced.

It is said that Emperor Franz Joseph, in signing these documents, would have said to Count Apponyi: "I hope that from now on the process of 'Magyarization' will become more efficient."[50]

We should also remember here another law from 1875 and modified on 5 May 1891 according to which all children younger than three years old should be taken away from their mothers and sent to special schools where they should learn the Magyar language. We should also mention the fact that those who did not do what they were asked to had to pay a large fine.

As for the high schools, in 1915 there were only 5 in the Romanian language for a population of 4,000,000 inhabitants. The requests by the Romanians to establish new colleges at Arad, Caransebeş, etc. went unheard; but the Hungarian authorities were unyielding; moreover, they did not hesitate in the "Magyarization" of the already existing ones.[51]

Higher education was even more insufficient: there was only one university in all of Transylvania and it was a Magyar one.

The Romanian language was excluded not only from education, but also from public administration. Justice was dispensed in the Magyar language by Magyar judges. Because of this there were many cases where no one understood the judges' decisions, this after they had to listen to everything in an unknown language. Many times the judges rejected cases which were not formulated into Magyar. Justice in these instances was a mere formality, if it was not refused altogether. This was in direct violation of the law of 1868.

Professor H. Gaidoz, former principle of the high school in Paris and an expert concerning the problems of Hungary, wrote the following lines concerning these deeds:

---

[50]This happened the very moment the emperor himself, in June 1848, had written: "I promise the Romanians a constitution adequate to the real necessities of this people, in accordance with the future of the monarchy..." adding, one month later, "You can be certain the just and legitimate requests of the Romanians will be met."

[51]The Romanian Bishop Vulcan, to give an example, gave the Romanian community in Beiuş the necessary funds to build a school. After having overcome the Magyar opposition owing to some "higher" intervention, the school eventually began functioning. Obviously, the classes were given in Romanian. The Magyar authorities could not tolerate this "Wallachian" school; thus, ignoring the law of 1868, and despite the constitutive act of the school, dated 1851, specifically stipulating that instruction will be in Romanian, the Magyar authorities did not hesitate in obtaining an order from Budapest forbidding instruction in Romanian under the threat of closing the school permanently.

The imposing of the Magyar language is a very serious problem, not just because language is a symbol, but also because it is the expression of nationality, and that is why the Magyars wanted to impose their language on all the nationalities in Hungary.

We do not have to compare Hungary, a very small and diversified state, with a state like France where the language and the nationality were imposed in provinces of different origins. The only state in Europe to which Hungary could be compared is Switzerland with its four nationalities and four languages. But there is a very big difference: in Switzerland none of the nationalities (not even the German one, which is superior in number to the others) claims to oppress the others. The imposing of the Magyar language is not just an oppressive one toward the other non-Magyar nations in Hungary, it is also a new thing and Hungary cannot evoke "this historical right" of which the Magyars are so fond. If the Hungarian state could survive throughout the centuries without being disturbed by the enmity of its nations, this is due to the fact that the languages of these nations were the so-called "vulgar" languages of the Middle Age, the opposite of the educated people's language, Latin. Latin was the political, administrative, and juridical language of Hungary; it was an accessible language for everyone but also a neutral one. It was Hungary's official language until 1848; Latin was spoken in the Parliament in Pest until 1848. The Magyar language that became the official one in all departments turned into a permanent offensive against the non-Magyar nations of Hungary. The Romanians demands were not different from those of other nations subjected to the Magyars, but they were also excluded from all the administrative functions in the provinces where they formed the majority of the population; they were treated as strangers in their native territory.[52]

The persecution against the freedom of the press. Even if laws guarantee freedom of the press in Hungary, for the Romanians, for almost 30 years, it did not exist. The penal code, art. 171, an old law out of usage, "the imperial document from the 27 May 1852" and art. 13 from 1893 give the Magyars the right to use their weapons against any Romanian revolt and to force the Romanian nation to keep quiet.

The law from 1893 was very efficient; it was against "any kind of action that could threaten the constitution and the unity, independence,

---

[52]Gaidoz, *Revue de Paris*, 15 May 1894.

and integrity of the state or against those who did not want to use the official language."

"There was," as Scotus Viator says, "a very precise and also a very evasive formulation, that the authorities could do whatever they liked against those who did not want to give up their nationality."[53]

In Transylvania, being a journalist is not a very well-paid job. The journalist risks in every moment his own freedom and life. To publish a newspaper you must pay, before everything, a very large sum of money that should cover the trial expenses and the convictions that will surely come. For any news article that appeared after the law of 1893, the judges had the right to accuse the article's author and the editor. The trial could be judged by any other jury outside the defendants' district of residence and the members of the jury were selected carefully from the greatest Magyar patriots. The results of these proceedings are easy to guess.

From 1880 to 1886 the Magyar juries judged 36 trials against the Romanian press. Of 86 defendants, 66 were found guilty and served prison terms from 15 days to 5 years and had to pay penalties of thousands of francs.

In the past 20 years things worsened; Romanian journalists have been convicted to more than one hundred years in prison and forced to pay fines of 250,000 crowns. To understand these accusations, we should note that before 1895 the greatest part of the trials against journalists were conducted before juries in Sibiu and Curtea, made up exclusively of Germans, where Romanian journalists were often acquitted, a fact which led to the moving of all trials from Sibiu to the Magyar Court in Cluj (Ministry Order no. 31482 from 27 June 1885). The Romanian press felt from the beginning the results of this change.

We will present some of the convictions of Romanian journalists. Let us first look at the famous trial of the "Memorandum" that awakened the interest of European public opinion.

In 1887 the Romanians, because of the endless list of accusations against them, protested in Sibiu where a "Memorandum" was written to present all the claims and rights of the Romanian nation in Hungary.

This document, written in Hungarian, German, and Romanian, and conceived in a very elegant manner, was to be presented to Emperor Franz Joseph.

---

[53] *Op. cit.*, p. 14.

Three hundred public figures went to Vienna for this reason on 28 May 1892. This delegation exercised its rights under the law. Because of demands by the Hungarian government, the emperor refused to meet the Romanian delegation or to receive their "Memorandum."

While the delegates were in Vienna, their houses and families had been mistreated by the Magyars, and they were harassed upon their return.

The leader of the Romanian National Party, Dr. Rațiu, was threatened with lynching and had to leave Turda for Sibiu. A public prosecution was quickly initiated against 25 members of the Romanian committee in the court in Cluj where there were many Magyar nationalists.

The jury was carefully selected. "I saw then," said a foreign journalist present at the trial, "procedures that would not be allowed in any other civilized state: lawyers who were not allowed to defend their clients, who were in turn made fun of and insulted by the jury, evidence favorable to the defense that was deliberately misunderstood or mistranslated from Romanian into Hungarian, judges with a totally cynical attitude."[54]

Almost all of the defendants were convicted: Dr. Lucaci — 5 years in prison. Dr. Rațiu — 2 years, Prof. Comșa — 3 years, Dr. Coroianu, Berceanu, Mihail, Patița, and Domide — 2 and a half years, Pop de Băsești and Velcico — 2 years, Suciu — 1 and a half years, Cristea — 8 months, Patriciu — 2 months.

European public opinion was revolted by this monumental injustice. "This trial was a shame on the Hungarian nation," wrote Georges Clémenceau on 12 May 1914.

Leading European politicians publicly condemned the medieval policies of the Magyars. Important protests were signed in support of the convicted Romanians by the following: Jules Simon, César Cantu, Björsten Bjornson, Pugliese, Vte. E.-M. de Vogüe, A. Naquet, Lavisse, Rambaud, Giosue Carducci, Macias y Rodriguez, Leroy-Beaulieu Vandal, Frédéric Mistral, Flourens, Clémenceau, Henri Rochefort, Accolas, Lecomte de Lisle, Levasseur, François Coppeé, Emile and Paul Dechanel, Émile Zola, T. Leveillé, Sully Prud'homme, Arthur Meyer, Georges Fazy, Hugo Lavenga, General Parmentier, the University Youth from Paris, Geneva, and Rome...[55]

---

[54]See *Le Phare d'Alexandre*, 6 June 1894, *Journal des Débats*, *L'Aurore*, *Temps*, *Revue de Paris*, *Revue des deux mondes*. *Nouvelle Revue*, etc., of the time.

[55]The signatures of these personalities have been reproduced by Professor V.A. Urechia, former minister, in an album entitled *Voci latine*, București, Socec, 1894.

Written protests were addressed to political figures in Vienna and Budapest, discreet interventions were made to Ballplatz by nations friendly to Romania and Austria. All of these efforts were useless and the convicts remained in the Magyar prisons.

Hardly had this situation passed when another Romanian writer, Aurel C. Popovici, was arrested and condemned to 4 years in prison because he had published a work in which he presented the history of Transylvania and protested against the Magyar policies concerning the other nationalities. Romanian journalists who supported their fellow countrymen were also convicted: Slavici — 1 year in jail, Ion Rusu Şirianu — 11 months, and Roman and Balteş also went to jail.[56]

This is what Hungary meant by the liberty of nations and freedom of the press. The list of convictions and persecutions is too long to be recorded here, but all this happened before the eyes of the whole of Europe which tolerated these kinds of deeds in the middle of the nineteenth and early twentieth centuries.

The abolition of the right to free association. These rights on which European nations in the West pride themselves and for which the human society has fought for centuries, the basis of every democratic society, and which are basic to any liberal policy, were denied to non-Magyars, and especially the Romanians, living in Hungary.

Any association, of any kind — professional, artistic, or for mutual assistance — was forbidden; attempts to organize literary or artistic associations failed in Lugoj, Caransebeş, Cluj, Braşov, etc. because they were denied authorization from Hungarian officials. Examples of this policy are: the *Opinca Română* literary society; *Minerva*, the student literary society in Cluj; *Progresul*, a society in Arad; the Romanian women's societies in Cluj and Satu Mare; the cultural society of Romanian teachers in Satu Mare; the society of artisans in Alba Iulia and Blaj, etc.

We must also point out that the freedom of assembly was denied to the Romanians in Hungary; to hold any kind of meeting the Romanians had to obtain permission from the Hungarian authorities. If by any chance this was granted, the police and the gendarmes, who assist at these meetings, had the right to interfere and to break up the meeting at any time.

---

[56] *La Revue hebdomadaire* in Paris, which opened an inquiry on the demands of the Greeks, Romanians, Bulgarians, and Serbians, compiled a huge list with the fines and sentences for the political crimes, disorderly conducts, and the wearing of the Romanian tricolor, given our by Hungarian Justice between 1901-1912.

Scotus Viator quotes the case of such a rally organized to support calls for "the universal vote" that was forbidden by the authorities because the organizers forgot to mention what kind of universal vote they would discuss. In 1914, on the eve of the war, a meeting in Alba Iulia, attended by 8,000 people, was interrupted by the chief of the local police when the gendarmes present there, even if they did not understand the Romanian language very well, told him that "the Romanian gentlemen who spoke at the rostrum incited the people."[57]

Sometimes the results were even worse. In October 1901, at Comanova, peasants gathered in the center of the village to clarify a problem concerning a local pasture were ordered to go home without any explication. When they refused to do so the Magyar gendarmes fired their weapons, killing three people; they arrested the others.

On 25 October 1901, at Voieslava (Banat), during a religious service, the gendarmes who decided to use all means to scatter the crowd, recklessly killed Ștefan Baba.

On 11/24 April 1904, at Lendi (Bihor), at 2.30 p.m., the gendarmes attacked and shot the Romanians who, being at a meeting of Socialists of different nations, refused to listen to the Kossuthist speakers, but, after their departure, they refused to go home: 56 bullets were fired and the crowd was attacked with bayonets, 30 people were killed, 30 seriously wounded, and another 100 beaten.[58]

We end this long list of examples, without any commentary. These deeds speak for themselves.

Persecutions against the Romanian Church. Despite the policy of "Magyarization," for more than 40 years, there was only one institution somewhat respected by the Hungarian authorities: the Romanian Church. But this did not last. Two years before the outbreak of the European war a special law was passed confiscating some of the Romanian churches in Transylvania and, without taking into consideration the pleas of the Romanian nation, turned them over to the Hungarian bishopric, which had been provisionally set up at Hajdu Dorog. Only the Magyar language would be used in these churches and only Magyars would attend the ser-

[57] R. Șirianu, *op. cit.*, p. 354.
[58] *Revue hebdomadaire*, 20 March 1915.

vices. The Romanian people in these areas, from this moment on, lost the right to pray in their native language.[59]

* * *

We cannot finish this review of the situation of the Romanians living in Hungary without mentioning a few other suggestive "cases," that should enlighten readers about the manner in which the Romanians have been treated for such a long time in their own land.

In 1886, a large amount of gold was stolen from the Buciumeni mines. To discover the truth and to punish the thieves, who were supposed to be Romanians, the suspects were suspended upside-down and beaten with ropes soaked in salty vinegar.[60]

The Magyar newspaper in Cluj, *Elenzek*, in no. 146 from 1887, published the following correspondence from Caransebeş:

> On 23 June, along the road to Orşova two gendarmes passed by in a carriage. A Romanian peasant was tied to that carriage; he had been forced to run behind the carriage for 5 kilometers and, when couldn't run anymore, he was dragged along behind it.[61]

During Easter, Hungarian soldiers shot to death Romanian peasants who protested against the profane insults by Magyars concerning their "savage" rituals. Instead of punishing the murderers, the authorities arrested the Romanians whom they held in prison preventively for many months until finally they were not found guilty. (Decision no. 3561 from 1889 of the Court in Alba-Iulia.)

On 23 April 1907, at Berechiu, the mayor Petru Pecsta was stabbed with bayonets by the gendarmes in front of the Magyar priest for protesting against his illegal act that wanted to force the children to speak Magyar in school.

9 May 1907 — Gendarmes killed G. Marcaş from Tinea and arrested many people accused of provoking disorder.

9/22 August 1907 — During the legislative elections, the gendarmes injured the peasant Drăgoiu from Beiuş who was dragged along the streets

---

[59] Şirianu, *op. cit.*, p. 346.
[60] *Les Roumains de Transylvanie, par P.C.* Paris, Pelluard, 1894, p. 5.
[61] Ibid., p. 5.

bleeding to frighten the Romanians who were intending to vote for Dr. Lucaci.

12/27 August 1907 — At Panade, near Blaj, the Romanian population was brutally attacked. Battalion 4 of the 24th regiment of Saxon soldiers was established in the village. At the end of a party at the Romanian school, Captain Iacob, being drunk, hit teacher Ion Bercea with his sword and then the peasant Leon Cipariu. Many people gathered in front of the school. The drunken officer ordered the soldiers to scatter the people with their weapons. The order was carried out and the peasants were driven away cruelly. During this action Ion Borcea Sorica was stabbed with a bayonet, two women had their bellies cut open, while the furious soldiers entered the houses and attacked the peasants. This was the result of that day: ten seriously wounded: professor Ion Borcea, father of five children; Ion Borcea Sorica, unmarried; G. Zorios and his wife Maria (five children); Leon Cipariu; Dumitru Câmpeanu's widow (five children); Ion Brașoveanu and his mother (three children); Maria Cipariu; Maria Z. Ciugudeanu (four children). Another 40 persons were less seriously wounded: Anton Irimie, Leon Cipariu — the son of Iacob, Ana Boldiș, Maria Dicoiu, Irimia Loghin, Vasile Bouar, Petre Brad, Nicolae Brad, Teodor Cipariu and his wife Ana, Nicolae Barbat's widow, Pavel Lupeanu, Valer Borcea, Vasile Salea, Ion Câmpeanu — son of Augustin, Traian Luceanu, G. Ciuguldeanu, the mayor Al. Posa, Dumitru Aldea, and other ten persons. There were only 200 people in the entire village. The "official" investigation found that the soldiers acted in self-defense; the persons listed above attacked the battalion with "Manlicher guns and bayonets."

It is very easy to see that there are 5 women among the 10 people seriously wounded, also 10 women among the other 40 wounded, but not even one soldier was scratched during "this action organized by the Romanian peasants."

In September 1907, at Cristian (Brașov), a group of young people ridiculed a soldier who called his army comrades. They came with their weapons and wounded many Romanian people.

On 6 October 1907, at Pecica Română, a gendarme argued with a young man, then pulled his sword to fight him and his friends. Some other gendarmes also came with their bayonets. Ion Sicloveanu's left hand was cut. Ion Trif's head was cut open, another Romanian was seriously wounded in his neck, and ten other persons were injured.

It is useful to present some articles from the Hungarian press during that time, extremely interesting because of their tone.

The Hungarian newspaper *Kölösvár*, on 3 August 1891, wrote "Only brute force can impress this uncivilized mass [the Romanians]," and concluded "We must obtain the authority and power even to dominate Romania." This coming from a state that was supposed to be a friend and an ally.

The Hungarian newspaper *Szatmár*, on 28 February 1891, wrote the following: "This ferocious animal [the Romanian], cruel and savage, hates to death the Magyars and gnashes his teeth, so that he looks awful. We will throw you out of the country, you ungrateful and perfidious people. It you do not like our language, then go away. We do not need traitors. Go to hell, because the woods and the crows are waiting for your bodies."

The newspaper *Magyar Hirlap* on 22 September 1894 published the following: "It is a pity that the useful institution of impaling has fallen into disfavor. We could have used it to solve radically our Wallachian problem. And what a joyful spectacle it would be to watch the famous agitators [Raţiu, Lucaci, etc.] thrust on those spears dressed in their national colors!"[62]

It is unnecessary to continue with examples of this kind. It led Henri Rochefort to say: "...we go all the way to Béhanzin, under the pretext of stopping human sacrifices while such horrible acts are taking place only a few miles away!"[63]

We would like to think that the situation of the nationalities improved after the beginning of this terrible conflict created in Europe by the Magyar-Prussian coalition.[64]

---

[62]Brote, *op. cit.*, p. 113.

[63]13 May 1894.

[64]One of the Romanian officers serving in the Hungarian army wrote about the way in which Romanian soldiers were treated by the Hungarian officers, this at the height of the war:

"There were three active officers in charge of the organization of the battalion. The rest of us, all retired, were simply watching them. They were not deprived of difficulties. Two of them, both Hungarians, didn't speak Romanian, while the third one, who seemed to me to be Romanian, would seldom have the floor.

Captain Patakfalvi would speak Hungarian and when he commanded in Romanian, he would not manage to make himself understood, lost his temper, and did not hesitate to beat the poor men to an inch of their lives, with fists, kicks, and Hungarian curses such as *Diaszno olah, büdös olah* (swine of a Wallachian, Wallachian rot), the usual 'kind words' the Magyars overwhelm us with.

......Foreign officers molest the Romanian soldiers, brutalize them, and behave as barbarians. Let's skip the curses; no day passes without the Magyars finding a reason to beat them. Once a soldier received 25 blows on his back because he had used the officers' toilet; another one,

But the war has only provided an excellent pretext to destroy the best elements of the Romanian and Slavic nations. Thousands of Croatian, Czech, Serb, Slovak, and Romanian priests, teachers, and writers were arrested, summarily judged for imaginary crimes and punished, often being sentenced to death or prison.[65] According to some Austrian newspapers, up to the end of the year 1915, 3,873 Romanian and Slavic people were convicted and sentenced to death by war councils in Austria.[66]

The Magyars, more cautiously, avoided giving information on this subject; but a reliable Romanian source told a Romanian general who was leading an army during the Romanian occupation of Transylvania (1916) that, up to the time of Romania's entry into the conflict over 12,000 Romanians were sentenced to death by Hungarian councils of war.

Concerning the rest of the Romanian citizens, their problem was very simple: all the men between the ages of 16 and 50 were drafted and sent to their deaths in high risk actions along the front lines to be killed by Russian, Italian, or French gunfire, in places where Hungarian troops would not dare to go. In this way nine out of ten Romanian troops were sacrificed from the beginning of the war.

---

who refused to offer water to a sergeant, was struck in the abdomen with a boot; one caught while stealing uncooked potatoes was arrested and beaten; he was from my company; I was ordered to give him 25 blows, but he got off with two nights on duty and I also gave him a pair of slaps, formally, as an example for the others. To none that the officers have a real hatred against our people.

There is a gap between the officers and the soldiers. It is a dreadful hatred. The Hungarian officers, irritated that Romania did not join their side, take out their rage on the peasants; they often bear them with a bull whip and at night they show off with the torments they use on them; hunger, non-stop duty; the pillar (to which they are bound) are the lightest punishments.

The soldiers who report, as newly arrived, or to make a request, whatever it may be, must do it exclusively in Hungarian. Before the war, it sufficed to utter the beginning formula 'Captain, I obediently inform you that...' the following being done in Romanian. Now. during the war, they find themselves compelled to know, all of a sudden, Hungarian. Those incapable of memorizing Hungarian sentences in the report are bound to the pillar for two hours, even in wintertime. I happen to know two of them who were dead by the time they were released; I am sorry I did not write down their names. I saw officers beating soldiers black and blue for not speaking Hungarian. One day a Hungarian officer stopped a Romanian soldier wearing the tricolor rosette on his peaked cap on a street in Cisnădie; he snatched the latter's peaked cap, tore the rosette, threw it on the ground, trampled it underfoot, and slapped the soldier. (Oct. Tăslăoanu, *Trois mois de campagne en Galicie*. Paris and Neuchàrtel, Attiger frères, 1916.)

[65] See, on this matter, the valuable statements of professor G. Beck of Bern in his work. *La responsabilité de la Hongrie*, Paris, Payot, 1917, p. 17.

[66] Şirianu, *op. cit.*, p. 420.

Leonte Moldoveanu, a lawyer and teacher from Transylvania, now a deputy in the Romanian Parliament, has exposed, from the rostrum of the House of Deputies in Bucharest, this attempt at the extermination of the Romanian nation:

> The Austro-Hungarian political leaders tried to destroy the Romanian nation in Transylvania. For this reason, the 23rd brigade was always sent into the most desperate battles. It took part in so many assaults that the others mocked it, calling it the "Vorwäerts [forward] brigade." All of its members were Romanians. Today, it no longer exists because it was slaughtered during these endless and pitifully glorious attacks.[67]

No one could stand it any longer!

Any further patience could be seen as a sign of complicity on the part of the Romanian government which could be suspected of desiring Transylvania "without the Transylvanian people."

Of course, no one could accuse the Romanians that they ever wanted to conquer the territory of another nation and of not being patient. At the same time, no one could deny that their national consciousness, forever

---

[67] Here are some illustrative pages, written by the same former Hungarian Lieutenant Oct. Tăslăoanu, cited above:

"We stop at the entrance of Staremiasto. We are joined on our way by Regiment no. 5 Seghedin, formed of retired soldiers, with tricolor ribbons attached to their peaked caps and chests: they are true born Hungarians. They have not fought, so far, in any battle. From Halici to here this is the first Hungarian troops that we can see and they are intact; otherwise, we met only Romanians: Transylvania moved to Galicia. It is obvious that Tisza and the High Austro-Hungarian Headquarters keep on applying even on the battle fields their extermination policy toward the minorities. It is not accidental that Galicia is full of Romanians...

...The cholera cases were increasing dreadfully. We are warned to avoid in particular regiment no. 24, retired; there are hundreds of ill men. No preventive measures are taken at all and the ill men are not quarantined; so much the less is the problem of vaccination raised. The doctors are angered by the attitude of the military headquarters. They all come to report to the brigade chief. General staff Captain Homolya, an exacting and cruel Hungarian, answers 'it is all the same if the regiments from Transylvania die under the Russian bullets or from cholera.'

Our brigade is commanded by General Henner, a weak man, almost a puppet in the hands of his assistant. Captain Homolya, an ambitious and petty mediocrity.

It is obvious this man sought to exterminate us by all means, otherwise one cannot explain the orders he gave.

Our regiment, formed of 3,500 men, lost 170 of them at Havay. In the 2nd Company, which numbered 267 when we left Făgăraș, there are 5 men left, 6 including me."

untainted, made many Romanian patriots think of the reunification of ancient Dacia. However, the government and Romanian leaders in Transylvania, wanting peace in Europe above all else, were afraid to encourage these hopes. On the contrary, both sides made efforts to calm spirits, hoping that one day the Magyars will see the reality and will commit themselves to respect the rights and freedoms of the other nations in Hungary.

During the disputes in 1883, Professor Urechia, president of the Association for the Cultural Unity of all Romanians, declared in the Romanian Senate that the Romanians in the kingdom only seek for their brothers the right to develop their own language and nationality:

> ...our goal is not liberation from Magyar domination, but only a reconciliation between the Magyars and the Romanian Committee from Sibiu and for the former to recognize the rights of the Romanians concerning their own nationality, not as being against the Hungarian authorities.

These were the ideas supported by all Romanian political leaders. The speech in the Romanian Senate on 27 November 1893 by Liberal Party leader D.A. Sturdza, at that time the opposition leader, characterized Romanian policies as being very wise. More than this. Count Kálnoki, at that time Hungarian minister of Foreign Affairs, agreed twice (on 18 and 19 September 1894) to requests of the Romanian government in Bucharest in front of both Hungarian and Austrian delegations.[68]

Not even the Transylvanians were thinking differently than their fellow countrymen in Bucharest.

Eugen Brote, former vice-president of the Romanian National Party of Hungary, in his remarkable work about the problems of the Romanians in Transylvania and Hungary, mentions clearly: "...all these troubles exist only because of the aggressive policy of 'Magyarization.' It they decided to apply in Hungary the principle of equal rights for all nations, all of this dissatisfaction would disappear along with the reasons that make impossible a sincere friendship between Romania and Hungary."

These ideas, common to all the Transylvanian people, were developed by Aurel C. Popovici (one of the Romanian leaders in Transylvania),

---

[68] See Jehan de Witte. *15 ans d'histoire, 1866-1881*, Paris, Plon. See also the speech by V.A. Urechia, translation by L. Lévéque, Bucureşti, Göble, 1894, as well as the speeches and most important documents gathered by E. Broté at the end of his work *Voinţa Naţională*, previously quoted, published in Bucharest, 1895.

in his remarkable work called The Romanian Problem in Transylvania and Hungary published in French, German, Romanian, and Magyar in 1892.

Popovici asked:

"What exactly do we ask for today? Do we ask from the Magyar something that is not rightfully ours? Do we ask for privileges? From 1848 until today we, the Romanians, have not been asking and do not ask for anything but that which is ours; we want our national rights, even if we live in Hungary, because we want to live here, we asked for these according to the juridical principle *suum euique*; we want to have our own leaders and judges, to speak our own language, and to create our own national cultural institutions; we ask that we should decide our own fate, and we will never admit that the Magyars tell us what to do, what to think, what to speak, and to rule our lives.

In a word, we want only one thing in this world: our own country; we want to be the owners of this land that for centuries has been inhabited by our parents and ancestors; we want to see this sun called national liberty! This is why the whole Romanian nation, young and old, ask for the right to live as a nation on our own territory.

We are a people who realize our own national value and dignity; we are brothers by blood and language with the Romanians in a sovereign country and, as God is our witness, only death can take away from us the nationality of our parents!

The Romanians ask to be a free nation in Hungary having the same rights as the Magyars...

Consequently, while the Romanian nation would not be recognized as a free one, having its own autonomy concerning its administrative, juridical, and intellectual problems, we cannot speak about peace between the Romanian and Hungarian peoples.

Once, a long time ago, the young Magyar people said that they would like to be friends with the Romanians.

This is a good thing and we want this too, but between slaves and masters friendship can never exist.

The young Magyar people will think this way as well because this friendship can be built only on one basis: national freedom![69]

To these loyal and sincere words, the answers of the Magyars were insults, beatings, assassinations, and convictions.

---

[69]Popovici, *op. cit.*, pp. 7 and 147.

Popovici was convicted to four years in prison because he wrote the words you have read. But this was useless, being convinced that the Austro-Magyar policy against the Romanians and the Slavs was a real danger to world peace, he tried all his life to find a solution to this serious problem.

In a very amassing book, *Die Vereinigten Staaten Oesterreichs*, he suggested the creation of a United States of Austria, in which the autonomy of the nationalities making up the Hapsburg Empire would be recognized. His model was inspired from the constitution of the German Empire. He called for the creation of one parliament elected democratically in each state, in accordance with their own institutions, customs, and needs, federal finances, a central parliament, a superior chamber and in each state an executive power headed by a responsible government.

If Popovici had been listened to, Franz Joseph could have been the greatest emperor of Austria and the wisest sovereign of his time. He could have gathered all the nationalities together and in this way he could have attached some other nations to his monarchy.[70] He could have saved the European peace and his tired empire would have been the center of a New World.

"If he [Popovici] had been listened to," wrote Charles Andler, the chance of peace could have been greater, without causing any damage to Austro-Hungarian ambitions."[71]

Not only was he not listened to, but his book was banned in Hungary and Popovici was forced to leave the country.

Popovici was not listened to, not were the Magyars such as Déak, Stephan Zeckeni, and Ludovic Mocsary who opposed this violent policy of "Magyarization" which they considered "utopical and unfair." They thought that this kind of policy would provoke the kind of disaster we have witnessed for these past three years.

The loyalty of the people to Franz Joseph and their wish for reconciliation were so obvious that in 1914 they suggested it once more to the Hungarian government and wrote a list of requests for Count Tisza who, they believed, would not refuse them. Their called for:

— the application of the nationalities' law, forgotten after 1868;

---

[70] For this matter concerning the Serbs and the Yugoslavs, see G. Beck, *op. cit.*, p. 105.
[71] *Le pangermanisme*, Paris, Collin, 1915, p. 76.

— the changing of the electoral process so that the Romanian population would obtain its own members in parliament;

— the repeal of Count Apponyi's laws regarding the Romanian schools;

— the appointment of Romanian civil servants in the Romanian regions.

Such a program could not have been denied by any other nation but Hungary. Magyar chauvinism rejected the Romanian claims and this was the death sentence of the Hapsburg monarchy.

* * *

After examining all of this evidence, clearly showing how the Romanians sought to ensure their fundamental rights, how can they be accused of exaggerated ambitions? Can the Romanian government be accused of having an aggressive policy or imperialist tendencies when these were in fact the policies of its enemies?

Would it have been better for it to sit by and watch all of these assassinations, convictions, and brutal "Magyarization" to which almost a half of the Romanian nation was subjected without protesting in anyway? We should ask the Germans, the Magyars, and the Bulgarians what their attitude would have been if half of their fellow countrymen would have suffered persecution of these sorts in a foreign country, such as the Romanians had to suffer in their own land.

This is why the Romanian government could not stay out of this international conflict, this is one of the causes that made them take the side of the Allies, and this is why King Ferdinand of Romania, even after the sad events caused by the defeat of the Romanian armies, had the courage to say these words that now belong to history: "...if I had to do this all over again, you can be certain that I would."[72]

---

[72]Interview in *Figaro*, 20 April 1917.

Chapter II

The Second Reason for Romanian Intervention: The German Threat

We have spoken until now of the suffering of the Romanians in Hungary, we have shown their multiple and unfruitful attempts to convince the Hungarians to change their policies, we have also mentioned that today both the Romanians and the Slavs unanimously concur that they cannot find their salvation without a victory of the Allied armies in this war. Well, we dare to state here, to the great honor of Romania, that this country could have still hesitated to intervene in this frightening struggle, if it would not have understood that a less selfish and more powerful duty was calling it to the side of France, Italy, and England: the duty to fight against the German threat.

Nevertheless, the political and economic situation of Romania has never been more promising than during those last years.

The major part of our national goals appeared that they could be realized without any sacrifice, without shedding a drop of blood on our land, and all this while realizing enormous financial benefits by offering wheat, oil, and gas (following the example provided by other European countries) to the highest bidder.

It seemed Romania should just follow the advice given by the Iron Chancellor in 1868 "to maintain good relations with all your neighbors and wait, patiently, for the ripe fruits of the European tree to fall by themselves on the table..., to maintain good relations with both sides and, as a last resort, if everything else fails, to join those forces whose victory seems certain."

If it had answered the kind invitations frequently repeated by the Central Powers, even in return for simple neutrality *usque ad finem* Romania would have received back Bucovina, unhoped for liberty for the Transylvanian Romanians, many favorable frontier changes at various locations and, in case of a victory of the Central Powers, the land of Bessarabia, once Romanian, always Romanian, the richest soil in Europe, larger than half of Romania. But Romania did not accept these proposals and preferred to enter the war, with the enormous risks that war implies, and that it knew this war would imply.

Of little importance was the moment Romania entered the war; the important thing people must remember is that, despite seeming hesitation, as soon as Romania understood the German threat, it opted decisively to enter the conflict, accepting all the risks and suffering it implied.

* * *

It is useful to study the evolution of this country's sentiments during the first months of the European war. We will not mention France. Those who know Romania are acquainted with the long lasting and endless admiration that this nation feels toward its elder Gaelic sister.

From the first moment of the war, Romania was, with its heart and soul, fully on the side of Marshal Joffre's soldiers. The achievements of France were its own achievements, France's dreams were its own dreams; nowhere in the world is France better loved than in Romania, which, as a wise man once said in a public conference, "is the French colony that is best linked to the mother state and which took the least blood, the least money, and the least labor."

Hence, we will not mention again Romanian sympathies for France, but we will examine only Romania's feelings toward Germany.

Despite difficulties and his narrow spirit, Germany, before this war, was, if not loved, at least highly esteemed in Romania.

That great enterprising spirit of the Germans was admired, which, unfortunately, we have not had the opportunity to find in the French or English peoples; their great organizing spirit was admired, which Europe appreciated, at its full value, even during this war; Germany was also admired for being the land of Beethoven, Bach, Goethe, Schiller...

Without taking into account the events of 1870, the Germans remained for the Romanians the inhabitants of the shores of the heroic Rhine, of the beautiful Rhine which starts at Coblentz and ends at Rudesheim, of the Rhine from *Legends of the Rhine* by Heinrich Heine.

This war has shown to the Romanians, as well as to the entire universe, that the old Germany exists no longer; that the generation of blue-eyed dreamers and philosophers, aspiring to the conquest of the pure rationality, has died, and that in their place a new, harsh, and fearsome nation, enlivened by a mad dream of world conquest has arisen.

This war has shown to Romanians they should read more carefully the operas, discourses, and songs that they considered to be the empty words of some philistine old men, to carefully research the new German mentality, and to become aware that the good God, who is love and mercy, the God of the humiliated and of the oppressed, was chased out of German temples and replaced by Thor, the wild god of the barbarian Germans, who brings hatred and disgust; that this entire generation of philosophers, historians, and priests are serving, unanimously, at the altar of the 'Force' raised to the rank of a new ideal, that this universal fraternity to which only yesterday these good "Welsh" ideologists still aspired is now the disgrace of the entire German nation which, through its teachers, politicians, and poets, spits with spite in the face of the whole world, its hateful words announcing the settlement of that *Kultur* by means of war, as the only instrument of progress, the regulator of human life, this indispensable factor for civilization.

Romania understood then that a great change had occurred in Germany, and that the affectionate Germany, built on dreams and poetry, had died, had truly disappeared.

It understood the meaning of Nietzsche's own words, who, when he encountered his former soul, wrote sadly: "It seems to me that I am a German from a dying species."

Romania understood that this new Germany which, through the voice of Lamprecht, Oswald, Haeckel, Bernhardi, places the "sword above the spirit" and sees in war the only source of welfare, progress, and even beauty, which finds that mankind without war is due to putrefaction (Lamprecht), which neglects and hates the oath of allegiance, peace, mercy, everything that is beautiful or good, which proclaims the establishment of the ideas of *Kultur*, *Realpolitik*, and *Realwissenschaft*. It was a Germany that Romania did not know. It understood, also, that this new

Germany whose ideal is no more than violence and vanity, was a danger for the world's future.

It understood, finally, as Lloyd George expressed it, that:

> If Germany would be victorious in this war, it will be dictating international politics. Its spirit and doctrines will prevail. By force of will, it will make spirits bend at its own convenience. Germanism under its most recent and harsh form will influence the philosophy and thinking of the world; if Germany wins, the dangerous spirits will be victorious in this war and we will then be vassals not of that good Germany, of sweet songs and noble and inspiring thinking, the Germany which wanted science to serve man, the Germany with a virile philosophy that helped Europe to break off the handcuffs of the superstition, no, not of that Germany, but of a Germany that used as a voice the harsh and tough roar of the Krupp cannons, a Germany that harnessed science to the carriage of destruction and death; a Germany practising a philosophy based on force, violence, and brutality, a Germany which, in its territory, just as in other countries, wants to extinguish, in a stream of blood, the smallest spark of freedom.

Is it not true that Germany, through the voices of its politicians, historians, and philosophers, proclaimed the end of the small countries?

Is it not true that a German, professor Lasson, proclaimed that "...a small country does not have the right to exist except according to its ability to defend itself..." and "between countries there is only one kind of right: the right of the strongest?"

Is it not true that another German, Daniel Freymann, in his famous book *If I Were an Emperor* wrote: "...small countries have lost, by their very smallness, the right to exist," that "a country cannot claim its rights to independence unless it is able to defend them with the sword...?"

And is it not also true that yet another German, but not any German, rather one of the best known, Treitschke, declared that small countries are a "phenomena against nature, ridiculous anomalies?" And that "the country is the power, and incapacity is contradicting itself while trying to express itself as a power?"

Which should be the responsible attitude of Romania, as a conscious member of the world community and one of the most important small countries?

Could a German victory not insure the success of the German idea and the principles discussed above? Is it not true that a German victory would have meant the bankruptcy of the principle of nationalities and the disappearance of small countries?[73]

The role played in 1913 by its "loyal ally" during the Bulgarian crisis enlightened Romania about the true feelings Vienna and Berlin held toward it. This war made the Romanian people aware of German desires in the East, consisting of dominating the Balkans, Turkey, and even India.

Given these facts, for Romania the choice was not a difficult one.

Our enemies tried to demonstrate the "immorality" of Romanian politics, accusing Romanians of opportunism. According to the Hungarians and the Germans, the Romanians hesitated for a long time to enter the conflict because they had the intention of joining the Central Powers at the moment when their victory seemed certain.

It is easy to demonstrate the absurdity of such allegations using documents that came from these very enemies.

In the first place, the telegram of 18 July 1914 of the Austrian minister in Bucharest, Count Ottokar Czernin, to Count Berchthold:

> The king told me that, in case Russia would be against us, we could not, unfortunately, count on the military support of Romania. By making this statement, the king was more emoted than ever and assured me that, if he could listen to his heart, his army would surely fight next to the Triple Alliance, but he could not do it.

This document of great importance was published in the *Austrian Red Book*, published in Vienna in 1916, p. 2, document 3.

---

[73] In December 1914, Take Ionescu, one of the greatest partisans of Romanian intervention on the side of the Allies, made a remarkable statement: "This war is a struggle between two ideals: on the one hand, the German ideal, that could be resumed to the cult of force, unaltered by sentimental considerations or by justice; this means the condemnation of the small states and the simple denial of the rights of nationalities, more directly speaking — making political and economic vassals out of the small; on the other hand, unexpected circumstances made the two Western republics (from the elevated point of view of the word, England is a republic) and the Eastern autocracy join together to fight for European freedom, in which the small nations will find their own freedom guaranteed and the possibility for their development according to the principle of nationalities...

Personally, I have nothing against Germany; I admire German patriotism, force, work, and national solidarity; but I cannot think of invading Belgium and of the ultimatum given to Serbia without being appalled with an almost physical resentment throughout my entire body!

I do not think that a citizen of a small state could help but understand that the authors of these two actions are his personal, irreducible, irreconcilable enemies."

A second document, of equal importance, is the great speech delivered on 9 November 1916 by the chancellor of the German government in the Reichstag Committee, where he states that on 29 July 1914 he telegraphed Vienna that he was "certain" that in case of war, "Romania would not join Germany and Austria."

Romania did not intervene from the very first days of the Great War because, unfortunately, as we will demonstrate, she lacked the technical materials required by modern warfare, and those who would become its later allies could not afford these even for themselves.

The fact is, though, that Romania chose long ago the path it would follow, taking into consideration its own interests, but also listening to that ancestral will that Gustave Le Bon calls "the nation's soul" and which directed it with all its energy to the side of its Latin sister.

We cannot end this chapter without pointing out one of the most beautiful gestures history has ever known: that of His Royal Majesty King Ferdinand of Romania.

German by birth, tradition, and education, he did not hesitate between personal feelings and duty. A few months ago, he stated:

> After we came to throne, the thought about the role Romania should play in the great conflict was permanently engrossing my mind.
>
> This was the great duty that I could not and should not run away from. How many struggles! How many fervent emotions! Since the beginning I imposed upon myself a conscience rule: to ignore my own self, my own origins, my own family, my personal feelings, and not to see anything else but Romania, not to think about anything else but it and for it. A monarch does not rule a nation for himself, but for his people! This, I think, is the virtue of a king. And I tried to remain faithful to it. When, step by step, after long meditations and reflections, I reached the conclusion that Romania's place was among the nations of the Entente, because they were of Latin blood and vocation; that its interests, not only immediate interests, but also permanent, historical interests, must place it next to France, Russia, England, and Italy; that by neglecting this mission it would become the same thing it has been for so long — a vassal to another power, and ruin everything that gives grandeur and nobility to a nation: national unity, liberty of action, independence... It was then that I felt encouraged because I saw, with certainty, the path to follow. But at the same time, I also felt a deep sadness because I understand that this path will take me forever

away from my family, my friends, my childhood memories... This was all happening inside my own self, please forgive these long words, I generally do not prefer them, but I cannot ignore them here, this was the struggle of my conscience and my heart. My conscience won, I imposed it on myself. My heart remained a little sad, and no one must blame it.[74]

Without any doubt, he no longer has feelings, parents, nor family in Germany, but this king who has sacrificed everything for the good of his people earned such an important place in history, in the heart of his people, and in the hearts of honest peoples throughout the world, that even his most brilliant ancestors would envy him.

While the names of many of the sovereigns of our times will be forever despised, his name will be pronounced, by future generations, with gratefulness and admiration.

* * *

It is very pleasant to see that the most elevated spirits of France, England, and Italy, understanding the ethical beauty of the Romanian gesture, immediately expressed their greetings to this people, and to the king and his government.

Therefore, Henri Béranger, on 10 February 1917, wrote, in the *Paris-Midi* newspaper:

It was not necessary for the Romanians to enter the war to gain advantages. Their neutrality could have guaranteed not only the salvation and tranquillity of life, but also would have surely brought benefits at the time the conflict came to an end. Rich in natural resources, independent in its own right, Romania preferred honor to security and duty to profits. She understood that Roman descent and its civilizing influence obliged her to take part in this struggle for justice fought alongside France, England, Belgium, Russia, and Italy. And, without retreating before ferocious enemy forces, she joined, with all her dignity, her flags and legions to our flags and legions.

René Pinon wrote in *L'Opinion* on 17 February 1917:

Before the great crisis, Romania lived peacefully and the people worked hard; it had been peacefully developing its institutions,

---

[74] *Le Figaro*, 20 April 1917.

organizing its economic life and building its wealth. The country was prosperous; its laws encouraged more and more peasants to become landowners. From Constanța they exported railway carriages with wheat and oil. Unexpectedly, the Great World War broke out, provoked by the German thirst for domination; Romania could have stayed out, to insulate itself in what President Roosevelt called "dirty content," but it understood that its affinities and honor did not permit it to stay and watch the fight where more than the material interests of the nation were put into play, the very moral patrimony of humanity.

Stéphen Pichon, former French minister of Foreign Affairs, also wrote in the *Petit journal* on 17 February 1917:

Next to the Belgians and Serbs, the Romanians are in the top of nations to which we owe, in the highest degree, our appreciation. They did not hesitate before the most terrible sufferings and the most cruel trials to tie their fate to ours and fight next to us.

These words are consolatory, especially during those hard times of great sacrifice and suffering.

Chapter III

Romanian Participation
in the European War

The entry of Romania into the war was one of the most important events of 1916. It generated great joy among its allies and the worst confusion among its enemies.

In Paris, Rome, London, and Moscow this event was received with great enthusiasm; in Berlin, Vienna, and Budapest, and other places, including Sofia, it was terrifying news.

To understand this, it is enough to quote the telegrams from that time:

Copenhagen — 30 August — the *Politiken* newspaper published very interesting details about the impressions in Berlin generated by the declaration of war of Romania.

The written announcement was released at 1:30 in the morning, when the newspapers were under press; these had to be content with the hasty printing of supplemental issues on separate sheets, announcing just the fact, without any comments. The news spread quickly, overnight, throughout the city and into the furthest neighborhoods. In contrast with Italy's declaration of war, Romania's struck like a lightning bolt on the people of Berlin, because, even if the possibility of such an event could have been foreseen, the idea of this having materialized, in an implacable manner, on every street corner, in large letters, seemed to grasp people in sight of the posters, giving them a feeling of frustration. Everywhere, in the streets, in tramways, omnibuses, an unspeakable consternation could be read on everyone's faces. The surprise was even greater among the people coming from the theater and among the regular clients of the cafés, who were talking in mad agitation about the new state of things generated by this event. The key political personalities do not even try to hide the gravity of the situation.

On 3 September, the polemist Maximilian Harden wrote the following in the *Zukunft* newspaper:

> It will not help if one tries to hide the gravity of the situation facing the Germans, Austrians, Hungarians, Bulgarians, and Turks. Their very existence is jeopardized, and the play will end in tragedy. If the enemy imposes his will, Bulgaria will be crushed, Greece will be pulled into conflict, Turkey will be encroached, Hungary will be dismantled, and Germany chased like a wild animal.

In Budapest, especially, you could hear nothing but screams and lamentations. The joy of the Allies, as well as the concern of the Central Powers, was fully justified.

Romania could indeed place on the first lines more than 500,000 soldiers, with 200,000 reserves; logically, its entry into the conflict could have meant the beginning of a general offensive on every front, the German impossibility to help the Hungarians, the crushing of the Bulgarians by the armies of General Sarrail joined by those of General Ivanov who could have crossed Dobrogea... shortly speaking, the end.

This impression was generalized also in the neutral countries.

Serge Basset speaks, in the *Petit Parisien* newspaper on 11 February 1917 about the emotion generated in Switzerland by Romania's entry into the war:

> in different circles the emotion was so great that one of the university youth leaders stated: "this event will mark an important moment in the history of people's liberation. In less than 3 months, the war will be over."

Unfortunately, this intervention was too hasty. Romania, from the very beginning of the war, just as France, Italy, and England, was surprised by events, not having any heavy cannons, nor enough ammunition, and lacking the diverse and complex war materials required by modern warfare. Germany knew this. Germany also knew, as we have shown before, that Romania was an enemy preparing for the battle, and thus, would have dashed upon it and its allies as soon as it would have received war planes, cannons, and ammunition requested from France, England, Japan, and the United States. For Germany, this intervention had to have as little chance of success as possible.

By the end of last spring, the Hungarians and Bulgarians were tired of war and expressed wishes for freedom that were dangerous to Germany. It was an emergency situation for the Germans to calm down these Hungarian and Bulgarian impulses.

Already wary of these "faithful allies," the Germans had to put before them a new threat to obtain, on the account of the help given to their causes, definitive and unconditioned obedience to the Central Powers. "The Romanian danger" was the perfect reason.

By casting a single stone, the German government wanted to hit two targets: to remove the Romanian danger, by rushing Romania's intervention before it finished its preparations, to overpower the "Hungarian megalomania" (of the *Madjarischen Grössenwahns*) and the summoning of the unreliable Bulgarians.[75]

Unfortunately, Germany kept its friends at the Petrograd court and used them to hasten the Romanian intervention. The Allies could not even think that Stürmer and his co-workers could play such an infamous role and associated with the Russian measures threats toward the Bucharest government.

We could say that the majority of diplomats and military attachés of the Allies in Bucharest, being informed about the real situation of the Romanian army, did not agree at all with the unexpected decision of the Russian government. There is a story about one of the military attachés of a friendly country, stationed in Bucharest at the time, bemoaning Romania's destiny.

One could say that the time of Romania's entry into the hostilities was chosen by the Berlin government, not by the one in Bucharest.[76]

---

[75]We developed this thesis in a long article printed in *Gazette de Lausanne*, on 6 April 1917. We are very happy to see that our theories have been confirmed, even by a writer, using the pseudonym of *Captain Iorder*, in an excellent work, *Germany and Russia*, recently published in Geneva by Atar Press (p. 17). Our opinion also seems to be shared by Professor G. Beck from Bern (*The Hungarian Responsibility*, Paris, Payot, 1917, p. 240).

[76]It is useful to repeat here the statement made on this issue by General Iliescu, former chief of the General Staff of the Romanian Army, to the press in April 1917:

"From the beginning of the Great War, Romania was sure that it would join the Allies. Already in August 1914, we began preparing and organizing the army. It was a difficult and time consuming task. From 180,000 men, our army should have reached 820,000 men, from which 500,000 fighting men. The officers should have been tripled. We did not have any ammunition,

We can fairly state that if the Romanian intervention was not what it should have been, this was due mainly to the maneuvers of the Russian government.

It has been demonstrated that these maneuvers not only hastened Romania's intervention, but also that the Petrograd government literally sabotaged the campaign of the Romanian troops.

The Romanian government has been assured about the Bulgarians not attacking the Romanians, but the Bulgarians attached Romania.

The Romanian government was assured of efficient help from the Russian army, but today we know precisely that the Russian government fought any initiative taken in this direction by the tsar himself.

Finally, the Romanian government was assured that it would receive all the necessary war materials from the very moment it entered the war, but, in December 1916, these materials were still delayed in railway sta-

---

not any machine guns. Do not be surprised by this statement: In July 1916, given the transportation and communication difficulties with our Western allies, Romania, despite the fact it worked ceaselessly, 'was not ready.' Although, around that time, from Russia we received a sort of ultimatum. 'Now or never' was the attitude of this document...

The Russian government presented us with a campaign plan completely elaborated; they did not take into account the probable role of Bulgaria. At our objection, Boris Stürmer, the prime minister at that time, answered that Bulgaria would never fight against Russia. Then we requested 200,000 men from the Russians for the Dobrogea front. He answered that 20,000 men would be more than enough for a purely political demonstration. In two rounds, our general staff asked the Russian government to begin an operation against Bulgaria, which would have been materialized by occupying a strip of land on the left bank of the Danube. The seizure of Rusciuc would have been a security link for our capital, but Russia rejected our proposals...

The defeat of Romania was foreseen and organized by Stürmer, who wanted to end the war by a sounding fact. Thus, in September, the Russian army was organizing along the Siret line, conscious of the events unfolding.

Here is what I think Stürmer was looking for when he forced our hand, when he organized our campaign: the seizure of Romania up to Siret, the recognition of the military power of the Central Powers, and then the conclusion of a separate peace as a result of the defeat, which would not have been a Russian defeat and, in consequence, would not have touched his or the tsar's power.

I conclude. We have been beaten because we were less armed than the enemy, whose command was clearly superior to our own, but the initial cause of our defeat was the disloyal plan of the Germanophile government in Petrograd, who played with the Romanian destiny to case a premeditated treason. This was an "imponderable" element which no Romanian, French, or English diplomat could have foreseen — this meant our destruction."

tions in Chișinău, Razdelnaia, and Kiev, their transportation being forbidden by Petrograd officials.[77]

This type of sabotage lasted until the fall of the old Russian regime, having a much more dangerous aspect: we now know that any important military information that reached Petrograd was immediately sent to Berlin.

Therefore, by knowing exactly what was happening on the Romanian front, the number of Romanian units, their movements, weapons, etc., the success of the German troops was assured.

Their task was facilitated also by the crushing superiority in terms of effectives and military materials. On 27 September 1916, General Mackensen stated, loyally, to the Berlin press agents: "Our repeated successes are due, before everything else, to the concentration of a strong heavy artillery...."

General Fóuville is not of the same opinion in the *La France Militaire* newspaper:

The young Romanian army was surprised, just as happened before, by the power of the German cannons. Either from the lack of time or lack of means to produce them or to buy them from abroad, it did not have, at the moment when it entered the battle, enough large-bore weapons. The successes of Falkenhayn in Transylvania

---

[77]Stéphen Pichon, former minister of Foreign Affairs of France, wrote in the *Petit Journal* of 26 June 1917, the following lines:

"This is not the time to insist upon the disastrous conditions in which the Romanian intervention took place, compromised from the very first moment by errors committed by others than the Bucharest government and donated, through Stürmer's betrayal, to the Austro-German armies...."

These lines, written by a personality like Pichon and published at the moment of the Balkan Conference Summit in Paris, are of great significance, historical as well as political. The well-known English writer Arthur Evans also wrote in the *Manchester Guardian* of 17 June of last year: "...today some know that the foreign help that the Romanian government was counting on has never arrived because of the conspiracy that took place in Petrograd."

On 28 July 1917, on the occasion of the ceremony which took place at the Sorbonne in Paris, when the flag of Stephen the Great was turned over to the Romanian Army, General Mallterre stated publicly, in the presence of the president of the French Republic, the members of the government, and the supporters of all the Allied forces, the following:

"Today we know what really happened. And we dare to state, in this very establishment, without denying the homage we owe to the Russian Republic and to the extraordinary uprising of its army, that Romania could not have foreseen in August 1916 the horrible machinations that was being knitted in Petrograd. Did the Allies know more?"

This betrayal, first denounced to the world by the author of this book, with the help of the Swiss press, can no longer be doubted.

and Mackensen in Dobrogea are due to the success of their artillery. The one-month wait of Mackensen, at a fortified position 20 kilometers south of the Constanța-Cernavodă line, had only one reason, to allow him bring the number of artillery pieces that he considered necessary. When he had them, he defeated the troops that held him position...

In the day that our Latin cousins would have the necessary equipment to silence the Krupp and Skoda howitzers and mortars, the equilibrium would be more than established. Only by sending the necessary means can the assistance of the great Allies be truly efficient. This problem of materials must be resolved.

In England, Russia, Italy, and France, the most authorized voices have been heard in choir stating that the Romanians could be helped in time. Last year's huge mistake in what concerns Serbia had too dire consequences and is all too present in everyone's mind, not to try the impossible to avoid its repeating.

The intentions of the Allies are thus very clear.

But what about the materialization of these intentions? To strengthen Romania with troops is a good thing. To strengthen it with artillery, even better. Heavy cannons, heavy cannons, and again, heavy cannons!

The Italian general d'All Ollio also stated:

Modern warfare requires an enormous amount of material. Cannons, medium-bore cannons, and especially large-bore ones, this is what all those who have been through the war request; and this is what we must continuously provide for them.

The *Times* newspaper correspondent in Bucharest wrote, in his turn, in one of the last October correspondences:

Romania needs not only to strengthen its troops, but also needs modern materials, heavy artillery, planes, armored cars which should be provided to allow it to fight from equal positions.

Is not this lack of anticipation, one of those "errors" for which the Romanian government is responsible? We do not think so. Today there is no mystery that the war has destroyed every principle that stood as a motivation for the arming of every nation in Europe, except Germany.

A couple of years ago, General Percin wrote in his book *Le combat*, published in 1914 (Félix Alcan, Paris), summarizing his own statements made before the Weapons Committee (p. 252):

If the Germans found it useful to raise the number of cannons in their army corps, this should make us happy, but do not let us imitate them; it would be madness to trouble the columns and battlefields with so many artillery pieces that there would not be enough room for the infantry.

On page 255, he wrote:

We have seen sooner how should one act in case of such cannons that shoot up to 7–8 kilometers and from which it could be enough to come closer by night, just as it happened in Viatressa, or to approach by day using covert means, to get two steps in front of them.

Regarding heavy artillery, General Percin wrote (p. 257):

Heavy artillery, among the qualities alleged in the 1910 regulations, remains only with the quality of shooting on curved trajectories.

And further on (p. 258):

Which purpose determined the Balkan nations to burden their campaign crews with such artillery? These peoples just wanted to do like the Germans, without asking if it was a useful thing to do or not. Will we do just like Balkan peoples? Imitating Germany must not be a rule for our governors.

At the beginning of the European war, as we stated before, Romania, just like the large majority of the European countries, did not have more than a light artillery, a campaign artillery. The heavy cannons dedicated just for some second-order operations, were present in the army just in a very weak proportion. Nevertheless, in the autumn of 1914, the Romanian government, realizing the sudden importance of large-bore cannons, contacted the French, English, American, and Japanese industries for the purpose of correcting this lack. Unfortunately, these countries' arsenals, for more than three years, were in almost absolute impossibility to send anything to Romania, given that France, England, and Italy did not have this war material for themselves in sufficient quantities, while America and Japan had already had signed some contracts with England and France. Only a few weeks before Romania entered the war could an important quantity of war materials be sent to Romania.

The major part of these materials has never reached Romania. Some of the transport ships were torpedoed by the enemy, while a considerable number of trains, loaded with planes, cannons, and ammunition, were stopped on their way to Romania by Stürmer and his partners.

It would, consequently, be unfair to accuse the Romanian government about this matter.

The Central Powers had on their side the secret of the Romanian operations, a crushing superiority in cannons, ammo, and planes, the advantage of a wonderful railway network, as well as perfect leadership unity

Their troops were, moreover, led by the best German commanders: Hindenburg, Falkenhayn, and Mackensen, to cite just the most distinguished ones.

Once war was declared, the Kaiser fired his old chief of staff and replaced him with Hindenburg.

Hindenburg, as chief of the German General Staff, immediately replaced the hesitating strategy of his predecessor with his own favorite strategy: he adapted the defensive on the lesser threatened fronts and a most violent offensive at those points where danger seemed to be imminent.

This formula was so elementary, we could say so classical, that Colonel Repington had foreseen this maneuver just from the beginning of our war, with an impressive precision:

> He will decide to keep on the defensive along the whole Russian front, in the north, and will concentrate all his offensive capacity on the Southeastern front, namely against Romania.

> For a new offensive of this kind the supreme German commander does not yet have the necessary forces: giving away Verdun, he could remove from the Western front 20 divisions of the 122 that were concentrated on the first of July between the North Sea and the Swiss border; he could take 4 divisions from forces concentrated around Vienna, and 4 divisions from the Italian front, thus putting together about thirty divisions.

> By following the path of least resistance, the Germans will try to decisively strike Romania, to conquer and crush it, just like they did to Serbia.

This prognostication proved as true as it was written!

Hindenburg took advantage of Russia's more or less conscious error of believing, once again, in the promises of the Bulgarian government, and first struck at Dobrogea. His task was easy, his army of over 100,000 men, with all its formidable war materials, attacked an opposing force of 30,000 men. Immediately after this success, having withdrawn troops from the other fronts, the numbers of which are difficult to know at the moment, but according to some information comprised 12 army corps supplied with an enormous amount of artillery, he turned with unprecedented violence against the new enemy to strike a finishing blow.

This was not an easy thing to do, because he encountered a determined enemy. With all his crushing superiority in men and materials, he could not gain land but step by step, paying expensively for even the smallest success. Only by repeated attacks with fresh troops on the same points could he defeat, at the cost of enormous sacrifices, the resistance he encountered.[78] More than once he was forced to change his plans, to probe, to retreat, to restart the fight; more than once he was forced to admit that he was defeated (at Jiu, Oituz, and Predeal, for example). The Carpathian passes and the Wallachian plain are soaked with the blood of his regiments.

Anyone who witnessed, even as a bystander, the struggles which continued incessantly for 4 months along the Danube, in the Carpathians, in Dobrogea, realized the heroism of the Romanian soldiers. By seeing the bravery with which he resisted the continuous assaults of the enemy, the flexibility of his maneuvers, his remarkable nimbleness, and especially his certain sobriety, one could appreciate his fine qualities.

Stanley Wascheburn, who witnessed these battles, had only elegiac appreciation for them. In the *Times* newspaper on 7 November 1916, among others, he praises the virtues of the Romanian soldier, his endurance, which he calls "perseverance in resistance," and his beautiful spirit, even in the most difficult moments.

Lacour-Gayet, a member of the Institute, described in the *Journal* of 9 March 1917, a moving picture of Romania's virtues:

> Since 27 August 1916, the Romanian army endured ten months of heroic battles. It numbers 450,000 fighting men, excellent soldiers, unparalleled in bayonet fighting, very resistant, because they all are dreadful peasants. They had to protect a 1,300 kilometer front which, excepting the Russian border, was threatened from every direction. Do we know what a 1,300 kilometer front means? It is the length of Russian Western front; but the Russians have there 1.5 million fighters. Our English-French front, from the North Sea to the Vosges, measures only 800 kilometers, and, on this relatively small length, how often do we have only 450,000 men?

---

[78]Général dc Lacroix, *L'effort de la Roumanie*. Paris, Alcan, 1917, p. 19.

This Romanian army, too weak for such a large front, performed miracles. For almost 4 months, without reinforcements, it held out in front of a force three times larger, well-supplied and having a formidable heavy artillery. It did not give up land without fighting step by step; it forced the enemy to obtain the land with the bloodiest casualties.

Falkenhayn decided to penetrate through the Vulcan Pass. Dragalina was defending this position of main importance. The Germans engaged a first division: it was decimated. The second division had a similar destiny. The third one managed to pass but things did not end there: back at the foot of the pass, at the small town of Târgu Jiu, a heroic defense was improvised: it was here that the scenes took place that will remain the pride of Romania.[79] The Germans withdrew from Târgu Jiu.

"Romania," writes General Lacroix, "was up to the level of its great allies. There was no sacrifice not to be assumed bravely to carry out the role it was assigned:"

> It placed its army, sons, goods, and future into Russia's hands. It stood bravely for a long time against more numerous and better armed enemies, astonishing them by its strength and long resistance..., it has shown to be worthy of its past and its noble, knightly brave traditions..., it is worthy of seeing the realization, in the future, of its legitimate national aspirations.[80]

* * *

Besides its indisputable moral value, the Romanian intervention on the side of the Entente powers had a positive effect, inflicting considerable losses on the common enemy. About 40,000 prisoners of war were taken by the Romanians. More than 150,000 soldiers were killed.

Moreover, without the Romanian intervention, the large forces concentrated by General Mackensen to the south of the Danube and apparently ignored by the Allies would have surely been thrown against General Sarrail's armies, whose fate would have been scaled.

Henri Béranger wrote:

---

[79]One single Romanian division resisted, without reinforcements, for 80 days against three German divisions, one of which, the 11th Bavarian, was completely annihilated.

[80]*Op. cit.*, p. 20.

When one saw, in a few weeks, the doubling of the effectives and the tremendous concentration of Falkenhayn and Mackensen armies that took place from the Carpathians to the Danube, to grasp Romania in a pair of steel pliers, one could consider that these armies, for a long time being ready, had a destination other than Turtucaia, Constanța, and Bucharest. And with all of General Sarrail's know-how and our troops heroism we cannot ignore the dreadful thought about the blow our Eastern army could have received under the sight of Constantine of Athens, if the Romanian intervention had not occurred at the right moment last autumn.

At the same time, there is no doubt about the great contribution of Romania's action in easing the task of the Allies on the other fronts. The Germans were counting on a too easy victory. The "punishment campaign" ordered by the Kaiser should have been quickly carried out. But the Romanians fought so bravely that the commander of the Central Powers was forced to bring a number of divisions from other fronts, many more than had originally been planned. The war correspondent of *L'illustration* wrote in the 6 January 1917 issue of this excellent publication that he had the opportunity to ascertain *de visu* the presence on the Romanian front of German and Austrian troops brought from Verdun, Riga, Somme, and Corso. The *Times* on 26 October 1916 wrote the same thing. The author of these notes also had the opportunity to talk, in the Romanian ambulances, to wounded German soldiers that came from Verdun and Gorizia.

Accordingly, we could state that the English victories at Somme and Ancre, and the wonderful French victories of Verdun, the Gorizia and Monastir seizure, were all due, at least partially, to the Romanian intervention.

In what concerns the indirect Romanian participation in the conquest of Belgrade, the *Genevois* on 18 March 1917 tells us:

We remember that on 27 August of last year Romania declared war on Austria-Hungary; on 28 August Germany declared war on Romania and on 1 September Bulgaria, in its turn, declared war on Romania. At last, shortly after that, Turkey followed Bulgaria.

What one does not know and the Russian press has told us, is that on 7 September a convention was signed between Germany, Turkey, and Bulgaria which stipulates the following: The declaration of war by Romania highly irritated the Kaiser, who was burning with desire to punish King Ferdinand, whom he considered a traitor. Thus, the German war council agreed to ask the Turkish government to send a powerful army to the Balkan and Galician fronts.

The negotiations unfolded quickly and on 7 September last year Germany, Turkey, and Bulgaria signed an understanding through which Turkey agreed to send ten new divisions into Europe, among them, three or four to Galicia and Bucovina, and six or seven to Romania.

The Allies, loyally and unanimously, admitted the important Romanian contribution to all these victories. The most precious homage we could present is the one accorded by the very enemy, General Falkenhayn, who, when interviewed in Berlin on 28 November by a New York Associated Press correspondent, several times gave the highest praise to the Romanian soldiers, stating "the desperate bravery that the Romanians demonstrated in repeated assaults is well-known by all German troops."

The career of the Romanian army did not end there. The remains of the army, joined with new contingents of troops, this time supplied with the necessary war materials, have formed a new army, of over 400,000 soldiers, which will soon have the opportunity to prove their virtues. From Iași we are already receiving the best news.

Albert Thomas, just back from his journey through Russia and Moldavia, declared, on 20 June of last year, to the London *Petit Journal* that "the Romanian army will perform miracles when Russia will give it the green light to start the battle."

"Oh! If only in Berlin," the *Temps* correspondent in Iași recently transmitted, "one thinks that the Allies are tired of war, the general staff of the Kaiser should become better informed using his numerous spies about the state of mind of the Romanian soldiers." Their country was, however, put through the hardest trials after the invasion, and they suffer waiting. They passionately await the communiqués from the front in France and when the troops advance there, they say: "*we* are advancing."

Many regions along the Moldavian border are again defended by Romanian troops and the day is not far off when the Romanian *dorobanț*, going forward, with his head held high, will add a new page to the glorious history of his country.[81]

---

[81] Amidst the Russian confusion, caused by Lenin's supporters and the corrupt elements in the German service, the troops of General Averescu, operating in Moldavia, between the valleys of Cașin and Putna, took over the offensive, broke the enemy lines creating a breach 60 kilometers wide and 18 kilometers deep, and between 24 and 28 July 1917 and confiscated from the enemy 98 cannons and took about 5,000 prisoners.

As a result to this heroic feat, the Romanian army received congratulations from the Allied governments.

Chapter IV

The Romanian Sacrifice

One will never be able to know the dimensions of the Romanian sacrifice for the cause of justice and freedom, all the more beautiful the sacrifice because it was freely consented to.

The losses and sufferings of Romania go beyond everything that was written and everything that was stated until now on this subject... and they are not finished. They can be compared to that of Serbia and far exceed those of Belgium.

The Romanian casualties numbered, up to May of 1917, more than 150,000 dead or wounded. Moreover, in December of last year the number of Romanian prisoners, declared by the German General Staff and officially announced by the Wolffbureau in a telegram on 13 December 1916, reached a total of 145,000. On 10 May 1917, the "War Correspondence in Vienna" (the official Austrian agency, Corr-Bureau) announced that this number does not exceed 79,033 people, of which 1,536 were officers, which leads us to believe that around 70,000 other prisoners had died in captivity as a result of epidemics, difficult living conditions, and wounds. The total number of casualties up to now would be approximately 220,000.[82]

But these are not all of the country's losses. Only at the end of the war will the real dimension of the losses become known. The greatest part

---

[82] A "Wolff" telegram from 11 July raises the number of Romanian losses to 300,000.

of the towns and villages on the former fronts in the Carpathians, along the Danube, and in Dobrogea were completely destroyed by enemy artillery fire and the invader's fury. The villages along the paths of the Bulgarian troops were devastated with a brutality and cruelty worthy of the sad fame these vandals received after 1912. Lieutenant C. of the Romanian auto transportation services, having had the opportunity to pass through these territories, depicted the most horrible image of the unlawful acts committed by the Bulgarian troops during their passage. After plundering everything in the towns, villages, and farms, after raping the women, cutting the children's bellies, and slaughtering the male population, these savages scorched everything.

The most odious theories of Clausewitz and Bernhardi were applied in Romania by its enemies, with a violence unknown elsewhere except, perhaps, only in Serbia.

During the battles preceding the seizure of Turtucaia the troops of General Mackensen, Bulgarians in their great majority, set out to commit acts of cruelty on the Romanian prisoners and wounded that exceed the human imagination. Soldiers and officers, like Lieutenant D. from the 75th infantry regiment, Captain C. from the 80th infantry regiment, who had miraculously escaped from this slaughter, depicted scenes that surpass in their horror the most spectacular atrocities described by the chroniclers of the Middle Ages. The wounded had their eyes torn out, their tongues cut off, their teeth knocked out, their skull scalped; those who were begging for mercy had their ears cut off, their genitals pulled out, bellies torn to pieces and stuffed with soil while they were shouted at "Here, dogs, have some land!"[83]

---

[83]Article 4 of The Hague Convention Rules provides that:

"Prisoners of war are under the authority of the enemy government, not in the power of the individuals or troops which captured them. They must be treated humanely. All their personal belongings, except weapons, horses, and military papers, remain their property."

And article 23 emphasizes:

"Except the prohibitions stipulated through the special conventions, it is strictly forbidden:

c) to kill or hurt an enemy which hands over his weapons or, not having any means for defense, gives himself up benevolently;

d) to state that no one will be spared;

e) to use weapons, shells, or materials to cause useless destruction;

f) to unfairly use the parliamentary flag, the enemy's national flag, military signs, or uniform, as well as the distinctive signs of the Geneva Convention;

g) to destroy or to take the enemy's properties, except in those cases where the destruction would be imperiously required by the necessities of war..."

Those described above are just a concise portrait of the terrifying acts to which Mackensen and his staff assisted, impassive and approving. Far from trying to repress these abuses, the high command had the extraordinary cynicism to stimulate publicly the savage instincts of its troops. Through a general order on 14 September 1916, immediately published by the Swiss newspapers on 15 September, General Jekov ordered his troops "to show the filthy enemies that the Bulgarians know how to be cruel." He also gave them the order: "without mercy, without any compassion." These unlawful acts will forever stain the honor of those generals and the memory of these crimes will remain forever attached to the folds of the flag they serve.

If the soldiers suffered such atrocities, the civilians, including women and children, did not have a better fate.

The enemy refused to take notice of the very clear text of article 25 of the Hague Convention statutes, signed, in the name of His Majesty Kaiser Wilhelm II, by Baron Marshal von Bilberstein, which states "it is forbidden to attack or to bomb by any means, towns, villages, houses, or buildings which are not defended." From the very day after Romania's intervention, a zeppelin overflew Bucharest, which was not defended; an important number of shells were thrown, causing material damage to civilians, killing women and children.

Such raids were repeated, ceaselessly, with the same effects, almost every night until the Germans entered the city.

On 26 September 1916 the author of these pages witnessed a scene more horrible than those told before which proves Heine was right when he said that the Prussian bayonet had killed all human feelings in the German soul.

It was afternoon, the closing time for shops, schools, offices, and institutions. It was a wonderful sunny day of autumn dawn.

...People crowded the sidewalks on the main street in Bucharest and the neighboring streets, where the large stores, banks, and public institutions are found.

Suddenly, amidst the crowd, the terrifying sound of an explosion could be heard followed soon by another and yet another and then by another two. The crowd was astonished; then, crazed with the realization of what was happening, rushed into the houses, courtyards, and cellars...

It was a terrible panic, full of dreadful cries, of screams of pain, of tram-pling underfoot... At the place where explosions occurred, in pools of blood were laying tens of inanimate bodies of old people, women, and children, jumbled together, forming unshaped masses of split skulls, torn chests, arms ripped off bodies, crushed legs... German planes choose to bomb this city — we repeat — the most crowded streets, at the time when they were filled with workers, children coming back from school, and old people...! Such scenes repeatedly occurred for three months, almost daily, and sometimes four, five, even six times a day. And this happened also over less important towns, over villages, even in the fields, uselessly, without any military purpose, serving nothing else but the pleasure to kill, the pleasure to cause pain.

These are things the Romanians cannot forget.

Yes, Maurice Muret was right when he wrote: "Until yesterday admired, if not sympathized, Germany does not awaken today anything but a sort of fear made from deceptions and hardly controllable disgust."[84]

Yet the bombs did not yield enough victims. Something more was needed.

It has been noticed for some time that the village roads and even those in the open fields were sprinkled with all sorts of "lost objects." Either chocolates, candy boxes, cookies and so on, or pencils, pens, hand-kerchiefs, even clothes for men, women, and children — to put it briefly, an entire bazaar which the passers-by hurried to pick up. Some of them, very scrupulous, especially adults, took these objects to the police officer or the mayor in their village who placed them among the lost objects, waiting for their owners to claim them; others, mostly children, ate the candies, chocolates, and cookies... and took home the pencils, the hand-kerchiefs, and so on. In a few days it was noticed, with stupefaction, at first the poisoning of those people who touched those cookies or can-dies, and later, epidemic diseases in those families where such objects were brought. The alarmed officials increased their vigilance to discover the people who were "losing" such dangerous objects and they sent samples of these objects for examination to the chemical and bacteriological labo-ratories of the government. It was found that those objects were "lost" on the public roads both by planes flying at a very high altitude, as well as by Germans and Hungarians whom the Romanian government, with its well-known kindness, did not place under special surveillance. The scientific

---

[84] *L'Orgueil allemand*, Lausanne, Payot, 1915, p. 344.

expertise was even more conclusive. It revealed authentic microbial cultures of tetanus, anthrax, cholera, and typhoid fever.[85]

As for the pens and pencils, they contained, without fail, explosives, capable, if not of killing people who would recklessly manipulate them, at least of severely injuring them. And who could still dare claim that this is a calumny? The author of these pages has had the occasion to see a whole collection of such "lost articles," at the Police Precinct in Bucharest last October.

People in the king's circle in Romania claim that the death of Prince Mircea, the youngest son of the king, which occurred in November of last year as a result of typhoid fever, would have been caused by these "candies" from the Prussian pilots. The *New York Herald* provides the following details about the prince's death:

> Some of the candies fell in the palace garden, the child ate all the candies he found and immediately fell ill. Investigations have been made, a few other candies were found, and the analyses demonstrated that they were infected with typhoid germs. That is how *Kultur* has been fighting!

As for the manner in which the Central Powers fight the war against Romania, King Ferdinand issued, in December of last year, the following statement to the *Times* correspondent in Bucharest:

> In a great war, which it seems will last at least one more year, a small country is fated to suffer enormous sacrifices and be drained of its resources. But the faith in its Allies was and is so great that it binds its own fate to their fate.
>
> Serbia and Belgium entered the war without knowing how the Central Powers would behave towards them. Romania does not make any illusions, because it knows the enemy will do anything to erase it from the map of Europe, as it did to Serbia and Belgium. The enemy is thirsty for revenge against Romania, because it dared to follow the path of justice and fought for the freedom of the Romanians in Transylvania; all this became clear from the very first months of the war. Bucharest has been bombed ceaselessly by zeppelins and planes; hundreds of women and children were killed and

---

[85]Tubes containing these kinds of microbial cultures were found in houses occupied by the German legation in Bucharest. The representative in Bucharest of the United States government took part in this investigation, as well as various journalists, among them Robert de Lezceu, the correspondent of *Figaro* in Romania. The article he wrote and published in *Figaro*, as a result of these findings, is one of the most enlightening.

mutilated while walking on the streets in our towns, without any defense. For the righteous decision of the Romanian government, the enemy took its revenge on the innocents. The effect of these actions was huge: the enemy has created an attitude that has solidified against him the entire nation and made impossible the acceptance of any peace without victory. The same attitude was obvious against the other countries that entered the war against the Central Powers.

When Romania was occupied, the Germans, forgetting once more the treaties and conventions, proceeded to arrest and expatriate the Romanian personalities who had remained in Romania. A substantial number of manufacturers and businessmen, lawyers and engineers, great landowners, even women, were arrested without any reason, without any excuse. Some of these prisoners were expelled to Bulgaria, Hungary, and Germany, others are still in detention, being subjected, without any purpose, to the most awful treatment. People are subjected to endless outrages, and the Bulgarians, especially, commit atrocities against them.

Regarding private property, although articles 28 and 47 of the Hague Convention regulations stipulate that "It is forbidden to plunder a town or a settlement, even taken by assault...," the invaders set about to pillage, both individually and collectively, making the actual situation of the unfortunate inhabitants of these regions one of the most lamentable.

This state of things would not surprise us. An official telegram from 3 December, dated in Berlin and published in the Swiss newspapers of 4 and 5 December, warned public opinion announcing that: "the country's exploitation has been undertaken according to preestablished principles," namely those inspired from the writings of von Hartmann and von Bernhardi.

Bulgarian General Tantilov, delegate of the Bulgarian government to the German military government in Bucharest, recently confessed to the editor of *Onevnic* in Sofia that: "the military government ordered the confiscation of all agricultural products, of all the raw or processed materials, and, generally, of every product of the Romanian land."

Le Figaro from 28 January describes the situation in the occupied areas in the following words:

The Germans proceed to a systematic plundering of the Romanian lands occupied by them or by their allies, especially Wallachia.

The crops housed in silos were, of course, sent to Germany or Austria-Hungary and the stores were entirely emptied as well and the

Germans compelled the people to give away all their provisions. In many cases they forcibly entered private homes and took everything: furniture, lingerie, food, and so on, without paying any compensation.

The most atrocious famine today marks these regions which were among the richest and best-supplied in all the world. The inhabitants wander around through the villages eating leftovers and boiled roots. The mortality rate is awful.

Hundreds of homes were scorched, thousands others were demolished by artillery shells or for the simple pleasure to hurt or produce pain. The country is a desert and looks like a horde transgressed by barbarians.

When we were in Switzerland, we received, through covert means, news from Bucharest, which confirms the information collected by *Figaro*:

Famine, slaughters, plunder, expatriations, all these fell upon us; once the end of the winter comes the epidemic diseases begin to drain our dirt poor country. Oh! Our unfortunate country is no longer anything more than a graveyard...

The honorable Mrs. R., settled for a long time in Geneva, received news last April from her mother who remained in Bucharest, a venerable lady belonging to the highest society in Bucharest, news that confirms all this information.

Engineer A. from Bucharest, now living in Bern, recently received news from Romania and told us that all of his industrial factories were dismantled and took by the oppressor, along with the furniture, art objects, clothes, and furs which were found in his private home.

The state of these invaded provinces is so precarious, that Batocki himself stated, on 10 May of last year, to the Berlin government that: "...this country was completely ruined and that which could be still gathered is many times less than in peace time."

Le Temps, in its issue of 13 June 1917, provided following information:

The Germans and the Bulgarians are treating the people of Bucharest like slaves. The harvests, the cattle, all sorts of food, were confiscated and sent to Germany. The people live in horrible misery. Every day, hundreds of peasants starve to death. They cannot resist the misery and hunger. To these curses are added cholera and typhus...

At the beginning of April in Bucharest you could only find some basic necessity edibles. Thus, a kilogram of potatoes costs 10 francs instead of 10 centimes in peace time; a kilogram of onions or beans costs 2 francs. Fat costs 20 francs per kilogram instead of 1.5 francs before the war. The lemons are paid for with 3 francs each, but you cannot find them. A chicken, usually worth 2 or 3 francs, costs 40 francs. The low quality meat was priced at 7 francs on 7 April last year. A kilogram of butter reached 23 francs and the milk exceeds 3 francs a liter.

Officers of the German command, along with the city administrative staff, have confiscated, from almost all the private homes, the cushions, blankets, cloths, shirts, shoes, pillows, and all sorts of clothing, stating that these were necessary for the wounded; in fact, these things were sent to Germany.

The manager of the oil and fat matter factories in Germany, a certain Küner, who lived in Bucharest before the war, chose to live in the house of Mr. Brătianu, the minister of War. The German military club settled in the house of the former Minister of Finance, Mr. Costinescu. The Bulgarian military club holds its gatherings in the Capşa Hotel.[86]

And for their "activities" not to be controllable and for the beggared people not to be able to complain or to find any defenders, the German authorities, after forbidding postal and telegraphic traffic with the occupied provinces, asked the representatives of the United States and the Netherlands who remained in Bucharest after the invasion to be good and leave the city, their place being in Iaşi, where the government to which they were accredited can be found. Obviously, these were disturbing events.

The Romanian sacrifices are even greater. Beyond the two rich crops, totally destroyed or confiscated by the enemy, which valued more than a billion, another great fortune of Romania, the oil derricks in Wallachia, were completely destroyed.

This campaign of destruction cost Romania over a billion francs. Over 80,000 wagons of kerosene and gasoline were scorched in ranks and refineries. Thousands of derricks were destroyed. Over 70 refineries,

---

[86]A neutral, Georges Oltramare of Geneva, recently returned from Bucharest, in a very "neutral" article, published by the *Journal de Genève* on 8 July 1917, said that "they cannot be blamed for anything else than the plundering of some abandoned houses and some isolated crimes..."

among which were the "Steaua" and "Astra" societies, the most important in Europe, were burned. The balance could be established approximately as follows:

Crude oil, gasoline, oils, etc.	75,000,000 fr.
Refineries	80,000,000 fr.
Tanks and tank cars	25,000,000 fr.
Derrick material stocks, etc.	100,000,000 fr.
Derricks and machineries	800,000,000 fr.
Total[87]	1,080,000,000 fr.

At the moment of printing this document, *Le Temps* from 2 August announced that the German, Hungarian, and Bulgarian troops, retreating before the Romanian troops, behaved just as they did in France during last year's retreat.

> When retreating, the enemy devastates the countryside. Every city is scorched, and the crops, the trees, even the bushes and fences are cut down and burned. This doleful show generates in the soul of Romanian troops an even greater will to win.

We did not exaggerate previously when stating that the fate of Romania is at least as tragic as that of Serbia!

To depict the entire dimension of Romanian sufferings, we must explain the significance of the withdrawal from the invaded regions, and especially Bucharest, and what is the present situation of the Romanians in the unoccupied regions of Moldavia.

Not to be suspected of favoritism and exaggeration, we prefer to use the reports of the *Journal* correspondent in Romania for the description of what this evacuation entailed (article from 27 January 1917):

> Although the Romanian capital, owing to its geographical position, was in constant danger from the beginning of the war, it demonstrated, as we said before, an unparalleled bravery.

> The city lived in a continuous state of alarm. Its local aerial defense was non-existent and, almost daily, it was bombed, either in daylight by planes or at night by zeppelins. The material damages were important and the victims very numerous. But the inhabitants got used to the danger so well that, without taking into account the police ordinances, at every appearance of the enemy planes, a compact crowd, attracted by curiosity, filled the streets.

[87] *L'Illustration*, 10 February 1917.

Any other calamity could not destroy the confidence until a bitter deception, caused by a false announcement of a great victory, deeply troubled public opinion.

Here we are, on Saturday, 25 November. Today, unexpectedly one could see the rumor spreading like a string of gunpowder, that during the preceding night an enemy division crossed the Danube at Zimnicea and Islaz.

They announced that the government ordered immediately the public administration and various ministries to leave, that same evening, to Iaşi, together with the diplomatic corps and the legation staffs. Throughout the town began a ceaseless movement of carriages and luggage loaded trucks to the North Railway Station.

At six o'clock I assisted, at the station, at the departure of the legations and ministries staff. It was a wild confusion!

Everybody seems to have lost their minds. Some are sad and numb, others are nervous, gesticulating. The crowd is pushing and packing just as the enemy would have already arrived. At last, the special agricultural trains move, consecutively, and vanish in the night. Meanwhile, the craze spread to a part of the population of Bucharest. The lamentable and tragic exodus began of frightened people who left their homes and goods, fighting each other in the station, assaulting the rarely forming trains; some leave by cars, others by coaches, oxen carriages, even on foot; they can carry only some small packs and a few beloved souvenirs.

Those who had the painful occasion to witness this exodus will forever have before the eyes the tragic vision of this crazed crowd, formed especially of women, children, elders, wounded... travelling over fields and roads, already whitened by snow, without knowing where, straight ahead. From time to time, demoralized people could be seen abandoning this mad flight, sitting on the side of the road, hungry, trembling of cold, demolished, looking straight forward, with the eyes scrutinizing the emptiness... Who could ever understand the pain of thousands of innocent people that died of exhaustion, hunger, and cold, during this tragic flight?! Who could ever understand the panic of these small martyrs running away from an enemy they knew was ruthless?

And, once they arrived in Moldavia, this crowd rushed into the towns and villages, settling randomly in rooms, warehouses, attics, and cellars. Rich and poor, boyars or beggars, in this shared misery, wander about from gate to gate asking for a shelter and some food. Towns which before the war numbered 10–15 thousand people now doubled or even tripled their population. Iași, which before the war numbered about 50,000 souls, in December of last year sheltered about 150,000 refugees. Little by little, the food supplies began to run short, wood for heating was harder and harder to find, and, for the misery to be complete, dreadful epidemics appeared... At the time we are writing these pages, we receive alarming news from Iași: typhus and recurrent fever cause numerous victims among the soldiers and the civilian population.

Meanwhile, in Wallachia, the invader sets to work. After having plundered everything, stolen everything, sent everything to Germany, Hungary, or Bulgaria, after imposing war taxes upon each separate town, in the value of many millions of francs, after bringing the occupied provinces to the deepest misery, the invader imposes a new war contribution, valuing 250 million francs, thus violating both human rights and the Hague Convention! And their acts continue...[88]

The streets became filled with crowds; the curious stopped at the fences of the palace; the soldiers were surrounded by people, they were asked questions. Yes, some women threw bouquets of flowers, but they were Germans; in the crowd there were also some people who were speaking Romanian, but a broken Romanian, who were Jewish-Romanians. The Romanian inhabitants of Bucharest remained at home.

Even the attitude of great Germanophiles did not lack dignity during these sad events. The old Carp answered thus to a delegation of officers that arrived to pay homage to him for his political activity: "No one but me could have wanted more to receive you in Bucharest as friends. The destiny of my poor country did not allow this to

---

[88] To answer some of the tendentious news released by the Germans concerning the "reception" they received when they entered Bucharest, it is appropriate to quote here the account published in *Genève* on 8 July 1917 by the neutral Georges Oltramare, who had just returned from Bucharest.

"First of all, I must discredit the legend that the Romanian population would have met the enemy troops with flowers when they entered their capital. This is totally false. I am able to explain the stories about that day.

Around two o'clock in the afternoon, on 10 November 1916, when no soldier had yet appeared, three cars crossed Bucharest. Mackensen was in one of them. The victorious general wanted personally to ensure that everything was in order and that no danger would menace his men. A little after that, the first patrols arrived. In field dress, with muddy, dirty uniforms and sad faces, infantry men and lancers defiled under the heavy gray sky. Some of them stopped in the palace courtyard, others crossed the various city neighborhoods, singing some glorious songs with tired voices of sleepwalkers. No party, no triumph.

happen. Gentlemen, today everything is separating us. I do not want to be more than a defeated enemy." Titu Maiorescu, who died recently, was no less proud. Mackensen one day sent his deputy to him: "His Excellency wishes to speak to you and grants you an audience," says the officer. Maiorescu answered shortly: "Does His Excellency not know my address?"

Chapter V

Romania's Future

After examining the sufferings, efforts, and sacrifices of the Romanian nation, it remains for us to analyze, in this last chapter, what could be the future of this nation, taking into account all of the possibilities.

We believe we have demonstrated the causes for which the Romanians are fighting, which is the very cause of justice. Romanians did not ask anything more than freedom for their brothers in Hungary and the right to live and to develop freely. Its ideal is the same as that written by the Allies on their military flag and which was recently proclaimed again by the leader of the United States of America.

It is obvious that the realization of the legitimate aspirations of the Romanians, as well as those of the Italians and Slavs under the domination of the Hapsburg monarchy, will strike a formidable blow to "this old skeleton," to quote the words of an Austrian member of parliament.

But Austria-Hungary still seems to enjoy, unfortunately, great sympathy in both France and England.

In London, as well as in Paris, there are people who still believe in the legend of a knightly and liberal Hungary, of a Hungary "à la Kossuth," tightly bound to French civilization and capable, at the right time, to "throw off" its northern allies. Even recently, Maurice Barrès stood vehemently against "their supporters who are ready to present them as lambs chased by a wolf whom they will sacrifice."

We act as a sincere and devoted ally by denouncing these dangerous sympathies and demonstrating their senselessness.

Unfortunately, there are few people who are well-informed about the problems of Austria-Hungary. In France and England, and maybe even in Italy, there are persons, even political personalities, who believe that one day they will be able to separate the Austrian monarchy from the evil influence of the German Empire. This is a great error which explains the sympathies we discussed earlier. But let us not be deceived by illusions. The dual monarchy is in everything indebted to the Germans. As Anatole France said, "it is subordinate to the highest degree and in its entirety." No power in the world could remove it from under this influence.

Reading books and discourses on this matter over the past fifteen years by the most prominent political figures in Austria and Hungary would be extremely useful for those who are not convinced.

Julius Andrassy, the famous Hungarian statesman, clearly states, in his famous book *The Austro-Hungarian Compromise*, that the monarchy must move as close as possible to Germany, this being the only way to ensure it a bright future: "We do not have any reason to be afraid of social absorption by Germanism, nor of Germanization by state power..." (pp. 401, 454).

In December of last year, the same Count Andrassy echoed Prussian pan-Germanism by writing in *Pesti Hirlap*: "The present military situation corresponds with our political intentions."

On 15 May 1906 the deputy Franco Stein, even more explicitly declared in the imperial council in Vienna: "The dynasty and the Austrian state are completely indifferent to us. On the contrary, we have only one hope and one desire: for fate to finally bring about that which must occur, namely the dissolution of this state, and for the German people in Austria to be able to live, outside this state, a glorious life, under Hohenzollern protection."

The same idea is upheld with more grace and more energy, by the Socialist Daszynski, who, on 25 September 1908, declared: "When this old Austria will breakup, we will not shed a single tear on the monster's corpse."[89]

Very recently, the political party of Schönerer also declared that the sole salvation of Austria is "its entering the Germanic Confederation."

---

[89] See Charles Andler, *The Pan-Germanism*, Paris, Colin, 1915, p. 70.

One of the most important members of the present Budapest cabinet, Count Apponyi, head of the Historical Independence Party, famous for his wild chauvinism, developed, in his turn, in the December of last year issue of *Das neue Europa*, the same political ideas.

At last, just a few months ago, the young Austrian emperor thought it would be appropriated to provide us with a new argument from his side. Before leaving for Bavaria in June he received in audience the chiefs of the political parties of the monarchy and ordered them not to attack in any way the "Great Ally." "This alliance," he said, "is and will remain the fundamental basis of our foreign policy; Austria's security is tightly bound to it and anyone who attacks our alliance with Germany causes a severe prejudice to Austria itself."[90]

Only a blind man could persist in the fancy hopes of the persons we quoted previously.

A French reporter, André Duboscq, who lived for a long time in Budapest and came to know the Hungarians better than any Hungarian-supporter in London or Paris who have never crossed the "gorge" and never overcome the "fortresses," recently described, in an excellent booklet

---

[90]See *Le Temps*, 4 July 1917.

Count Czernin, in his turn, made an identical statement to journalists at the beginning of April 1917.

The great Hungarian daily newspaper *As Ujsag* commented on the Austrian counsellor's statements in the following terms:

"Count Czernin is the first minister of Foreign Affairs to make a most important statement to the journalists. He gathered 15 Hungarian journalists and 30 Austrian journalists in his personal palace, where he sat at the desk of Metternich which is now his own. From the beginning, he declared that he gives a great importance to his permanent contact with the Hungarian press. His speech did not plead for either peace or war. The only goal was to protest against any attempt to create discord between the monarchy and Germany. Repeatedly and very energetically, he emphasized that the alliance with Germany is absolutely firm and unshakable."

Another Budapest newspaper, and not of the least important, *Pesti Hirlap*, made a similar analysis:

"Lloyd George must understand that the goals followed by Germany, Turkey, and Bulgaria in this war are also our goals and it would be impossible to try to separate Germany from the dual monarchy. Between the German chancellor, the president of the British Council and our minister of Foreign Affairs, some communications took place. This exchange of ideas will continue, but will not end successfully until the cabinet in London will cease to look behind the Michaelis speech for annexing tendencies and when its opinions will no longer be based on the unreal and unattainable probability of a difference of opinion between Germany and Austria-Hungary. The monarchy is not Italy; far from us are thoughts of betrayal and hypocrisy. We will not abandon our ally and will resist until the end, as long as the acceptance of the peace conditions, commonly established, are not assured."

entitled *Hungary, Yesterday and Tomorrow*,[91] the true feelings of the Hungarians. This booklet contains information that is so precious and so enlightening that we recommend its reading by all supporters of the "two-headed monster."

To those who think that Hungary is a country "of French culture" on its way to pull itself out of German arms and fall into French ones, he reminds, firstly, the propositions of one of the present members of the government, Count Apponyi, who is considered, in Budapest, as "the great friend of France" (!) and who, as a Public Education minister, in October 1908, at the inter-parliamentary congress in Berlin, speaking to the Germans — keep that in mind, to the Germans, not to the French or English — said:

> We study you, we think we know you, and we are convinced that nowhere in the world are you better understood than here, in our land. The German genius is the most universal of all the geniuses that were given to peoples. If, one day, a man would fall down from Mars, and would ask me which language he must study to understand the intellectual life of mankind on our planet, I would definitely recommend to him the German language. Only knowledge of this language can ensure the comprehension of the universal culture, of the culture of all living peoples.

That is why the German language became, in Hungary, a few years ago, the only mandatory foreign language in the teacher's schools. Mr. Duboscq considers it his duty to remind his compatriots that a Hungarian, Count Andrassy, the father of Julius Andrassy, about whom we previously spoke, was the one who, in 1870, prevented the Austrian government from helping France; he also reminds us about another Hungarian, Koloman Tisza, father of the present Count Tisza, who declared in 1888 in his now famous discourses, that Paris is nothing but the capital of a rotten country with which the monarchy should have the fewest possible ties.

The *Corriere della Sera*, very well informed, stands up in its turn against such sympathies and does not neglect to inform the Allies about the danger of such feelings: "The Hungarians," writes the newspaper, "after contributing to the unleashing of the conflict, madly throwing themselves with all their forces into the war, having a special satisfaction to play, in the East, the role of an avant-garde of Central Europe. They will maintain this position firmly until the end. They know that on the results

---

[91] Paris, Bloud, 1916.

of this struggle depends the perpetuation of their oppressive domination over the Romanians and the Slavs, as well as keeping the influence they now have in the internal affairs of the monarchy."

Another excellent authority on the Hungarians and the Prussians and their politics, Maurice Muret, a Swiss citizen, wrote in *Gazette de Lausanne*:

> To bestow upon the Hungarians the intention of change, even very little, their requests to ensure a lasting peace, means not to know the spirit of this nation, which is seen as generous, but is best mainly at following its own interests. Undoubtedly, it desires the peace, because it is suffering from an economic slump which engulfs the central empires; but the peace they try to obtain is a Hungarian peace, as deadly to freedom and against justice as the German peace.[92]

The last supporters of Austria-Hungary in France, England, or elsewhere should know that the monarchy is on its way to conclude a customs union (*Zollverein*) with Germany, a union which is nothing more than the first step to another union, more important and more dangerous for world peace. This union is supported with such obstinacy by the most important politicians and the largest German and Hungarian bankers that it will soon become a reality, if, by the time the printing of this book is completed it would not already be a fact.[93] We think it is sufficient to state that the true mogul of the monarchy, Count Tisza, is the best suited to demonstrate that the economic union of these two countries could be already considered a fact.

To realize the exact dimensions of this event, we will quote from an article by the Hungarian sociologist Oscar Jaszi, one of the opposition leaders, recently published in *La Gazette économique des Empires centraux*:

> The talk of a customs union is only part of a much more vast and much more important problem, which consists in transforming the

---

[92]We recommend, among others, the materials written by Mr. Duboscq and Cauvin, on the same subject, two admirable issues published in the *Manchester Guardian* of 16 and 17 June 1917, signed by Arthur Evans, the book of R. W. Seton-Watson, entitled *New Europe*, the books by Seton-Watson published under his pseudonym Scotus Viator, already quoted in our work, and, on the dominant political ideas in Austria, the work of the Austrian deputy Alexandre von Peez, entitled *Zur neusten Handelspolitik*, Vienna 1898, as well as the one by Josef Freiherr von Eötvös, *Die Nationalitatenfrage*, Pesta, 1865, Roth.

[93]Mr. Duboscq asserts that this accord was already concluded on 26 July 1916. We have reason to believe that the accord was not signed, but that it will be signed very soon. Nevertheless, it will not be made public before the end of the war… and with good reason!

main Central European states diplomatic and military alliances into a solid and integral political union.[94]

In conclusion, it is evident that sooner or later this political event will occur and we will assist then at the flourishing of another German federation, not with 80 million people, but with 135 million people, which will allow the Prussian noblemen, the Hungarian magnates, the Budapest and Berlin bankers, and pan-Germanic elements to fulfill their ideals of universal hegemony.

If Austria-Hungary remains in its present conditions, the Hungarian-Prussian brotherhood, instead of receiving the deserved punishment for its crimes and being prevented in the future from harming the world, will emerge strengthened, more arrogant and threatening than ever. The dead sacrificed by all the Allies would then have the right to shout at the diplomats and statesmen: "You have betrayed us!"

But, let us admit the impossible and suppose that the Hungarians — seized with an unexpected renewal of the gratefulness to the France of the years 1848 and 1856 or convinced that the hour of punishment has arrived — would want to "negotiate" for the purpose of saving what they could. Is such a discussion possible? Might Austria-Hungary, even at the price of a separate peace, be maintained in status quo ante?

Let us forget, for the moment, about the pan-Germanic danger, to which Austria-Hungary is no more than an avant-garde, the Eastern pioneer; let us leave aside for the moment the Hungarian conspiracies and the responsibilities which the whole Hungarian nation must bear; let us leave aside, also, all of the engagements made by the Allies and not consider anything but the issue of world peace; then, let us ask ourselves: is maintaining the status quo capable of guaranteeing a lasting peace, for which the world committed sacrifices unprecedented in history, to which the most noble blood of nations has been shed for three years, at Verdun, Flanders, and Champagne, at Trentin, in Poland, in the Carpathians, on the Danube...?

No, the Hapsburg monarchy hides a constitutive vice, incompatible with liberty and its close relative, peace.

On the Hofburg Palace's frontispiece in Vienna one can still read this beautiful slogan: *Justitia fundamentum regnorum*, explaining to Austria its historical duty. It could not justify its existence but by the loyal fulfillment

---

[94] See Duboscq, *op. cit.*, p. 43.

of this principle of law and justice, considering the various nationalities from which it is formed. It should have had to reveal itself like Switzerland, full of affection and opportunity for all its peoples. It should have been a good mother, but was no more than a step-mother. Because it did not understand what its role and its only mission in the world was, it must disappear and the Hungarians must receive the "honor" of having hastened its collapse.

It is finished. From now on any peace is impossible. The dice have been thrown. Too much blood has been shed among the Austro-Hungarian nations, too many tears have been shed and false promises of reconciliation made for this to still be possible. The experience of centuries has taught the all too faithful and naive nationalities not to hope any longer for anything from the present oppressors.

Too many royal words have been deceiving, too many engagements have been violated, too many laws were torn underfoot for a single Romanian, Italian, or Slav heart to have any trust in their masters in Vienna and Budapest.

And to explain that even the charming words, lately preferred in *articulo mundis*, spoken by the young Austrian emperor are not sincere, and his unexpected love for "his peoples" will fade, just like many others before, we will cite the true exponent of the Hungarianism, the voice of the heart, which does not lie, the statement released just a few days ago by the factotum of the Austro-Hungarian Empire, the former president of the council, Count Tisza, who, at a grand festivity clearly exposed his political program, when he stated, without any reserve, that he has decided to strengthen the Hungarian state not by concessions, not by the new liberties promised to the people by its young emperor, not even by the fulfillment of the old law of the nationalities, but "by changing the criminal code, whose articles refer to the treason against the state, and insubordination, which must be made more oppressive, by strengthening state supervision and, to go further, by the direct influence of the state upon the schools and seminaries."[95]

We will cite also the statement made on 15 June of last year, in the Imperial Council in Vienna, by the German Representative Heine, who expressed his dissatisfaction that, in Galicia, "too few are being hung" among the representatives of the nationalities. These words which display

---

[95]Speech reported in all Swiss papers on 8 June; see especially *Le Genevois* journal of the same date.

hatred and despise for everything that is not German or Hungarian reflect the unanimous thinking of the Germans and Hungarians gathered under the Hapsburg crown.[96]

These words show what would be the fate of the nationalities after the war. Once the peace signed, the tyrannies against the nationalities, already announced by Count Tisza, will begin again with even greater terror. The situation of the Italians, Romanians, Croats, and Serbs will become worse. The troubles known in Europe before 1914 will restart with greater intensity, along with the persecutions and abuse generated by the hatred and unlimited chauvinism of the Hungarians.

If Austria-Hungary remains what it was before the war and still is, the world will not have peace for a very long time![97]

---

[96] *Le Temps* journal, on 4 July 1917, published the following telegram which supports our thesis:

"It is known that in the Hungarian parliament, Count Károlyi made a violent indictment against the Tisza regime, accusing it of being the author of the world war, bur the Hungarian deputies returned to their chauvinistic unanimity when the Romanians Șerban and Ștefan Popp protested against the injustices and political persecutions carried our against the Romanian population. Tisza violently chastised the Romanian deputies, telling them that they should be happy that they are still allowed to speak in parliament and are still alive. He added that the calumnious statements uttered by the Romanians prove that the politics of conciliation tried by him had failed and they must revert to the strengthening of the Hungarian state against the nationalities system.

Count Apponyi, the minister of Public Instruction and Religion, stated then, to the applause of the chamber, that he will take action to protect the state from the threat of the nationalities and, before anything else, he will severely control the seminaries for priests and normal schools for teachers, either to make them centers of Hungarian patriotism, or to eradicate them.

The president of the council, Count János Esterházy, felt compelled to declare openly that "no government, Austrian or Hungarian, will ever admit the outlook on nationalities as it is sustained by the Entente. By no means will it ever allow Hungarian citizens to determine their own nationality, and to cut the links that ensure the cohesion of the Hungarian state..." (See the contents of the debates as reported in Swiss papers on 6, 7, and 8 July 1917).

[97] I was writing these lines in July 1917. And how right I was! The Hungarians did not wait until the end of the war to restart with all their forces, their Magyarization activities.

A telegram from Budapest to the *Gazette de Frankfurt* on 19 August, noon edition, summarizes a memorandum which was addressed by the Hungarian minister of Religion, Count Apponyi, to the Transylvanian consistories of Orthodox and Unitarian rite.

The minister declared that he decided, in public interest, to place the Romanian language primary schools under state control. The measure will first be applied in Transylvania to hamper the development of anti-Hungarian propaganda. That measure was provoked by the "anti-patriotic" attitude adopted by numerous teachers on the occasion of the invasion by Romanian troops.

This unshaped pile of theories, this amorphous aggregation of different ethnic elements, artificially connected, by force or because of the lack of ability of politicians in the past, this spotted state which has never been anything but a permanent nucleus of agitation, which does not represent a nation, which does not represent even an idea, must disappear from the center of Europe.

Lavisse and Rambaud wrote, twenty years ago, the following truly prophetic lines:

> An idea, this is what the Austro-Hungarian monarchy lacks. The Hapsburg Empire has too often refused to admit and despised the moral forces and placed trust in material means, to the ecclesiastical gendarme and the public gendarme. Today, ideas are taking their revenge...[98]

One of the leading editors at *Journal de Genève*, William Martin, who demonstrated a special sympathy for the monarchy throughout this war, wrote in his editorial on 3 August 1917:

> Not very far off is the time when the Austro-Hungarian rulers could have been able, through intelligent concessions, to include within the monarchy any pan-Serb desires. Instead, they preferred to let things go until they became unsolvable. In front of this sea of blood, which extends around the Serb issue, we cannot abstain from thinking, that for the good of Europe and the happiness of the monarchy, Franz Joseph lived too long.

And, on 25 August, he added: "Neither Austria, nor Hungary will be able to save themselves. They have lost the secret of their happiness."

The politicians and diplomats of the Allied Powers should not hesitate any longer, and should not leave themselves rocked by empty illusions. They must no longer proceed, as in the past, when they searched for an easy peace, a too-easy solution to the most desperate problems they confronted at the time of the signing of the peace accord. Europe has enough experience to know that nothing is more dangerous for the future than some hybrid peace treaties, hastily signed by old diplomats, hurrying to

---

In the schools placed under state control, teachers will be appointed who know the Romanian language, but the language of instruction will be Hungarian. Religious education will remain entrusted to the Romanian Church.

Count Apponyi omitted to say how that measure will cope with the declarations made in Vienna concerning respect for the rights of nationalities in the Danubian monarchy. (*La Gazette de Lausanne*).

[98] *Op. cit.*, vol. XII, p. 212.

sign the "final protocol" and restart the thermal water baths or their flirtations. Enough with such peace treaties which do not bring content to anyone and which leave the door open to more conflicts and controversies!

If we really want to ensure a durable peace for the world, with the hope for it to become permanent, if we want to realize a solid foundation for Europe, founded, as they said at the beginning of the last century, on the respect for nationalities and on serving the general interest, we should use radical measures, the essential one of which would be the break-up of Austria-Hungary.[99]

"With respect to the method of the dismantling," writes Louis Léger of the French Institute, "it is one of the simplest: it would be enough to return to every nationality of the empire the land on which it has lived since its origins and which was, remorselessly, abused by the strangers."

Bohemia, Moravia, and Silesia should find their independence in the rebirth of the Bohemian Kingdom.

The Dalmatian, Slovene, and Croatian provinces should return to their Serb and Montenegrin brothers, united by their own will in a monarchy or confederation, after a previous settlement with Italy.

Galicia should return to the Polish Kingdom, which will live again, we hope, and we wish to them the grand days of old times.

Trenton and Trieste should go to Italy, as well as some points on the Dalmatian Coast after negotiating with the Serbs.

The two Austrias, Tyrol and Salzburg, will form a united, simply Austrian Kingdom, while the independent Hungary will keep its pure

---

[99] *Le Temps* of 10 July 1917 published the following:

"As the Austrian problem remains a struggle between the central authority, which is German, and the non-German nationalities which claim their autonomy, it cannot be solved but in a single way: by the breakup of Austria. To keep the Hapsburg monarchy they must give it a reason to exist and that reason cannot consist but in being a counterweight to Prussia. Charles I could be seated solidly on his throne if he could have as a rival Wilhelm II. Being his vassal, he goes down."

Commenting upon the declaration at the inter-Allied conference in Paris concerning the essential goals of the war, the Italian newspapers on 27 July 1917 affirmed that these goals could not be achieved without the dissolution of Austria-Hungary.

"It cannot be avoided," wrote *Corriere della Sera*, "the reiteration of the criminal aggression the responsibility of which is borne by the imperialism of the Central Powers, without dismissing the possibility for the accomplices to plot against Europe and the world. So the best way is to paralyze and to isolate the most powerful accomplice, who cannot be tamed, by reducing to powerlessness the other accomplice, no less guilty of crimes, achieving at the same time the awakening of the oppressed peoples, who will be, after centuries, the best title of glory for the Entente."

Hungarian provinces, between the present borders, between Austria and the Tisa.

Transylvania, Bucovina, Banat, Crişana, and Maramureş, whole Romanian lands, as we have previously demonstrated, should return to Romania.[100]

Only by proceeding in this radical manner can Europe again have a lasting peace, being definitively protected against the maneuvers of the Germans and those of their accomplices, the Hungarians and the Bulgarians.

Let nothing be spoken about conquest and imperialism. "Returning" does not means "conquering." "Conquering" means obtaining by force something that does not belong to you, and not of something that has been stolen from you. And France, Italy, Poland, Romania, and Serbia do not ask for anything but the return of what was stolen and kept only by force, without taking into account the free will of the subjected peoples.

After the touching Franco-Romanian ceremony that took place on 28 July 1917 at the Sorbonne, Alexandru Em. Lahovary, an active exponent of the Romanian government in Paris, in a highly motivating speech, included these marvelous words:

> The peace that we want, the only possible one, the only that is worthy
> of the dreadful sacrifices which we have made, is the one that will not
> allow anymore that mankind endure such catastrophes.

It has been said: "No annexations! No conquests!" and we say the same. There must be no more annexations. Alsace-Lorraine must not be annexed anymore to the German Empire. Four million Romanians must not be annexed anymore to Austria-Hungary. Neither you, not us, pretend any annexations when we ask for the return to their homeland of the Romanians who grieve under a merciless yoke, of the Alsace and Lorraine inhabitants who fought against their splintering from their French homeland. Neither you nor us dream of conquests. Does to return with all legit-

---

[100] Regarding the requests of the Romanians, the well-known English writer Arthur Evans wrote last June in the *Manchester Guardian* the following considerations: "We must understand well that liberation (the free election of the next government) can signify for the Romanians of the Austro-Hungarian monarchy nothing but reunion with their free brothers of the Romanian Kingdom" and, after describing the ordeals of those Romanians, he mentions: "Can the Romanians of Hungary be forced to deny their national king and be loyal to the Hungarian crown which they despise? Is it to be expected on their part to give up the union with their brothers, to accept instead a closer union with their tyrants?"

imacy to the possession of heritage mean conquest? And does the uniting of the sons and brothers mean annexation?

The creation of a strong Serbia and of a strong Romania on the Danube will mean the end of the pan-Germanic dream, represented by the famous slogan: *Drang nach Osten.*

The existence of a strong Romania of 14 million inhabitants along the banks of the Danube, of a Romania regenerated by the inclusion of the wonderful Transylvanian elements, hardened by the trials it just passed through, is a new guarantee for world peace and for the free development of Allied interests in the East.

The Danube problem is still open. The importance of this international river becomes greater and we now know what an important role this wonderful communications route played in the German eastern expansion plans. West European countries, unfortunately, neglected the Danubian politics. Awakened after this dreadful crisis, they will not repeat, we are convinced, their past mistakes, they will not use any longer their outdated methods and dull doctrines. They must learn to promote a more active policy in the East, counting on proven friendships.[101]

A Latin sentinel, strong and conscious of its power, at the banks of the Danube, is an imperious necessity. We could argue that any Allied influence in the East depends on the Romanian nation in the future.

A crushed Romania, weakened, despised by its neighbors, would mean the crushing of any French, English, Russian, or Italian policies in the Balkans; it would mean rewarding the disloyal policy of the Bulgarian tsar and of Constantine. We do not speak anymore of feelings, nor even of honor, we speak about vital interests and these will not reveal to the Allies any other formula than the one we have exposed.

---

[101] We know that the Bulgarians, as well as the Hungarians, still enjoy some sympathy — rare, but lasting — in London, as well as in Paris. We advise them to read a book entitled *Bulgarians Seen by Themselves*, Payor & Co., Paris and Lausanne, 1917, in which a Swiss doctor, Victor Kühne, gathered a considerable number of Bulgarian documents.

Appendix

While this book was under print, events have followed their course. We will mention them, in a few pages, to emphasize the most important events that concern, in a very special way, Romania.

The day before the Stockholm Conference, on the eve of presenting another peace proposal to the world, on the eve of launching a new war loan, Germany needed a new success.

Incapable, now, to gain victories on the Western front, Hindenburg – helped in his initiative by Lenin and Zinoviev, tried to obtain sad victories on the Eastern front. He would have had to choose from two objectives: Petrograd or Odessa.

The first one presented three problems: distance, climate, and the fear of awakening in the Russians the instinct of self-preservation by menacing their capital.

He preferred Odessa, which could have yielded a success capable of gladdening the imagination: the complete conquest of Romania, which would ensure Germany, at the same time, with a wonderful seaside, the beautiful Moldavian land, and especially that of Bessarabia, the richest and the most fertile land in Europe and maybe in the whole world.

After a thorough preparation, at the end of last July, an order was issued to attack along the entire Moldavian front.

Mackensen and Archduke Joseph attacked the Russian and Romanian positions, with their usual violence. But this time, the Austrian and German troops found before them troops that were better equipped than in 1916. Moreover, they could not count this time on the criminal help of Stürmer and Protopopov. This time the Romanians had the occasion to demonstrate to the whole world that their being descendants of Rome was not an empty story.

The battle engulfed the entire front, from Bucovina to the sea, and continued for more than a month; at the moment we write these lines, it has not yet ended. The Germans and their allies have thrown into the attack about twenty divisions, among which six were completely destroyed and another eight so heavily decimated that the high command was obliged to withdraw them behind the front.

While the archduke's troops fought on the whole rest of the front, Mackensen proposed to capture the Cozmeşti Bridge, cross the Siret, and, after splitting the Russian-Romanian army in two, to defeat these two fractions, one by one, and continue, before the fall, his march to the East, up to Odessa. The orders found on the Prussian officers who were taken prisoners did not leave any doubt about the general's intentions.

The fight entered a decisive phase on 8 August. Just as at Târgu-Jiu, one single Romanian division defeated at Mărăşeşti, after three days and three nights of continuous fighting, three German divisions.

On 12 August, the general, surprised by the resistance of the Romanians, engaged fresh troops in the fight, moving his target slightly to the west. Every attack was again repelled, with unparalleled losses. The war correspondent of the *Times* reported: "The mountain troops who were taken prisoners confessed that since Verdun they had never seen such a terrible fight, and that the 12th Bavarian division was almost completely exterminated..."

The second day, the fight took on the same violent character along the whole front. The Germans had, on the Mărăşeşti front, twelve divisions, and the Romanians an incomparably lesser number of troops. Mackensen's troops failed again, their every force being stopped against the Romanian wall. The losses, on the both sides, were enormous. The Germans have lost over two divisions, the Romanians almost a whole division.

On 14 August, after strong artillery preparation and asphyxiating gas attacks, the enemy renewed its attacks. It was again repelled with considerable losses. The 89th Prussian division was, in its turn, completely destroyed.

While these heroic struggles continued ceaselessly along the Mărăşeşti front, no less important battles were being fought at Focşani, at Suşiţa, at Caşin, at Oituz, at Târgu-Ocna... in short, along the entire Moldavian front. Everywhere, the Romanian troops, either alone or supported by Russian troops still uncontaminated by German propaganda, performed miracles of bravery. The enemy's efforts, everywhere, continued to fail.

On 19 August, three new Austro-German divisions, supplied with formidable artillery, attacked from the northwest of the town of Panciu. Attacking in successive waves, the enemies reached the Romanian barbed wire fences. These, under the very sight of their king, counterattacked with such violence that the overwhelmed Germans began to run. "The land," wrote the *Times* correspondent, "was covered with such a great number of corpses, that the air became unbreathable." Many hundreds of prisoners were taken.

This formidable battle continued with the same results and motivation along the entire front for another twenty days.

The courage and heroism of the Romanian troops, in various battles, battle the imagination. They suffered, without any hesitation, the most terrible artillery bombings ever seen up to now. The massive attacks, executed with extreme violence by the Bavarian and German soldiers, collapsed before the impenetrability and bravery of the Romanian troops who, inferior in number, fought with an unmatched self-abandonment. There can be noted the case of the heroic 32nd regiment whose officers and soldiers, leaving all their equipment and clothes, went to attack only in their shirts and defeated the enemy.

The mountain corps, which entered the battle for the first time, took by themselves over 400 prisoners.

The 11th Romanian mountain battalion, at the cost of the highest sacrifices, fighting against an enemy four times more numerous on the Mărășești front saved the Hill 334 which was of a great strategic value.

On the Oituz front, eight Austro-German divisions fought for ten days and ten nights against two divisions, without being able to defeat the Romanian resistance.[102]

We do not know what will be the end of this frightening struggle; it is, however, certain that the fate of the Romanian army, despite its bravery, depends on the attitude of the Russian army. Anything can happen, but, from now on, no one can doubt the honor of the Romanian army. Due to the strong and unforgettable support from France, the Romanians have demonstrated to the world that they are not responsible for last fall's mis-

---

[102]We presented this short narration using the official bulletins of the time, the notes published in *Le Temps, La Figaro, Le Petit Journal, Corriere della Sera*, and especially the materials sent to the *Times* by its war correspondent in Iași.

eries, and that they deserve, using Polibiu's words, "the most vivid gratefulness of the future."

Admiration proofs for the Romanian army arrives from all the directions; one of the most impressive statements was made recently by one of
the exponents of Russian democracy. We fully quote the telegram published in the *Times* of 20 September of last year:

> Dr. Jablonowsky, high commissary of the temporary government on
> the Southeastern front, spent a few days in Odessa, where he was
> called to resolve some matters concerning the food supply. Asked
> about the events on the Romanian front, the high commissary
> declared that Odessa and Crimea pay homage above everything to
> the bravery and the determination of the Romanian armies, which
> sacrificed with heroic grandeur for the shared cause, in order not to
> fall under German authority.
>
> "History," declared Jablonowsky, "will place them on the same place
> as the immortal heroes from Marne and Verdun, and the peasant
> soldiers, who fought one against five, under fire from the deadly
> large-bore shells, ceaselessly, to save from invasion what remained
> unoccupied of our Romanian allies' territory."

What greater homage could be paid to an army?[103]

The spirits of the troops are beyond any praise. The wounded wanted
only one thing: to heal rapidly to return to the front. Today they hare
the Germans, as well as the Bulgarians, the Hungarians, and the Aus-

---

[103] Behold, on the other hand, a beautiful narration of these battles, sent on 23 August by
the Iaşi correspondent of the *Times* newspaper and published on 30 August of last year:

"The great battle which lasts for three weeks on the South and Southeastern Moldavian
fronts is one of the bloodiest fights of this war...

The troops of the first and second Romanian armies proved a fight capability that brought
the admiration of every foreign officer. Most of the prisoners thought that they had been fighting
against the French.

The German communicates speak about 14 Romanian counter-attacks, on the same position, in a single day. It is obvious that the Romanian army pays expensively its successes, but the
German losses are much heavier than those of the Russians and the Romanians.

The Germans attack in compact masses, just like in the battle of Yser. In a village where
the Romanians counter-attacked, there were found 2,500 German bodies.

The first divisions used by the Germans suffered such important losses that they needed to
be withdrawn. On the other side, some of the Romanian troops were not withdrawn for 14 days!

The young Romanian officers, just out of school, distinguished themselves by their
unbeatable courage. The soldiers of a regiment attacked with their shirts sleeves rolled up and
without helmets, because of the heat, to be lighter.

trians. The enthusiasm from the front has raised even more the spirits of the civil population.

They waited for everything with calm and absolute trust. Among both the civilians and the soldiers the spirit of sacrifice and devotion to the national cause is very strong; what is remarkable is the very common sense of these peasant soldiers who explain in simple and beautiful phrases the absolute necessity of Romania's entry into the war and the necessity to fight until the last man for the liberation of their captive brothers.

The stubbornness of the Germans on the Moldavian front could be explained by their political goals. They wanted to seize all of Romania, to order, just as they did in Poland, the installation of a government of traitors. This way Romania too would be a part of "Mittel-Europa." Their calculations are wrong, because even if all the Romanian lands would be seized, the soul of the nation would remain untouched, and there is no doubt about this.

Maps

If Romania Had Not Entered the War...

If Romania had not entered the war, the two armies, led by Mackensen and Falkenhayn, concentrated in July in Macedonia and in Russia,
would have fought, one on the Salonika front and the other on the Russian front.

When Romania Entered the War...

The Romanian intervention forced Mackensen's army to retreat to form the Dobrogea front and forced Falkenhayn's army to defend Transylvania.

Selected Bibliography

The following is a selected bibliography of important English language works on Romanian history generally and Romania's participation in World War I in particular.

Antonescu, Ion. "Romania in World War I," in *Romanian Civilization*, III:1 (Spring-Summer, 1994), pp. 43–62.

Hitchins, Keith. *Rumania, 1866–1947*. Oxford: At the Clarendon Press, 1994.

Seton-Watson, R.W. *A History of the Roumanians from Roman Times to the Completion of Unity*. Cambridge: At the University Press, 1934.

Torrey, Glenn E. *Romania and World War I*. Iași, Oxford, Portland: The Center for Romanian Studies, 1998.

Torrey, Glenn E. *Henri Mathias Berthelot, Soldier of France, Defender of Romania*. Iași, Oxford, Portland: The Center for Romanian Studies, 2001.

Torrey, Glenn E. *The Revolutionary Russian Army and Romania, 1917*. Pittsburgh: Carl Beck Papers in Russian and East European Studies, 1995.

Torrey, Glenn E. *When Treason Was a Crime: The Case of Colonel Alexandru Sturdza of Romania*. Emporia, KS: Emporia State University, 1992.

Treptow, Kurt W., ed. *A History of Romania*. Iași: The Center for Romanian Studies, 1997.

Treptow, Kurt W., ed. *Romania during the World War I Era*. Iași, Oxford, Portland: The Center for Romanian Studies, 1999.

Index

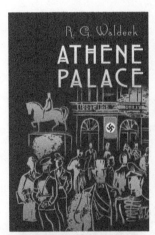
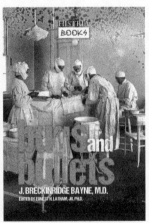

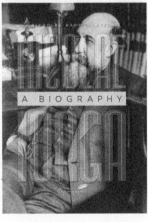